ORGANIZING SOLUTIONS
for Every Quilter

An Illustrated Guide to the
Space of Your Dreams

Carolyn Woods

C&T PUBLISHING

Text copyright © 2011 by Carolyn Woods

Photography copyright © 2011 by Carolyn Woods and C&T Publishing, Inc.

Publisher: Amy Marson

Creative Director: Gailen Runge

Acquisitions Editor: Susanne Woods

Editor: Liz Aneloski

Copyeditor/Proofreader: Wordfirm Inc.

Cover/Book Designer: Kristen Yenche

Production Coordinator: Jenny Leicester

Production Editor: Julia Cianci

Photography by Chanelle Richardson, Carolyn Woods, and Christina Carty-Francis and Diane Pedersen of C&T Publishing, Inc., unless otherwise noted.

Published by C&T Publishing, Inc., P.O. Box 1456, Lafayette, CA 94549

Library of Congress Cataloging-in-Publication Data

Woods, Carolyn, 1971-

Organizing solutions for every quilter : an illustrated guide to the space of your dreams / Carolyn Woods.

   p. cm.

ISBN 978-1-60705-196-1 (softcover)

1. Workshops--Design and construction. 2. Storage in the home. 3. Quilting--Equipment and supplies. I. Title.

TT152.W654 2011

684'.08--dc22

2010028181

Printed in China

10 9 8 7 6 5 4 3 2

ACKNOWLEDGMENTS

To my sister, Susanne, for this amazing opportunity. After admiring your craft for so many years, you got me in on the inside and then got me hooked.

To my husband, Kevin, and my children, Sarah and Justin, for all the precious time and quiet I needed to get this book researched and written. I love you.

To my biggest supporters in the writing process, Judy Westrum, Marcia Swires, Mick Williamson, Dave Stempien, Jamie Moilanen, Jona Giammalva, and Patty Macsisak. It means the world to me that you believe I can organize anything and then write about it.

To the ladies of Nimble Thimbles and of Calico Cut-Ups. You opened your studios to me without hesitation, answered even my most basic questions, and gave me so much to write about. Thank you to Jan for introducing me around, and then to Barbara, Becky, Charlene, Deanne, Emma, Gail, Jona, Marge, Mary, and Monica for your hospitality and for your infectious enthusiasm for your art.

To the extremely talented professionals in the quilting business who jumped right on board to be part of this book: Alex Anderson, Libby Lehman, Diana McClun, and Nancy Arseneault. I am motivated and in awe of your continued dedication to teaching and promoting the art of quilting. And to Mark Lipinski who, although we've not yet met, reminded me that quilting is more than a hobby. It's a lifestyle.

And to all the quilters, even the famous ones, who have taken the time to share their ideas and opinions with me in person and then on podcasts, in blogs, on websites, and in magazines. We all benefit from each other's organizing wisdom, efficiency tips, and storage savvy. You have all inspired me to give you my very best insight and encouragement to be happy, organized quilters.

CONTENTS

Section 1: Get Organized (The Overview)

CHAPTER 1: THE PROCESS OF GETTING ORGANIZED: A STEP-BY-STEP GUIDE

CHAPTER 2: ROOM DESIGN

Section 2: Storage Options (The Nitty-Gritty)

CHAPTER 3: FABRIC STORAGE

CHAPTER 4: THREAD, NOTIONS, TOOLS, AND MORE

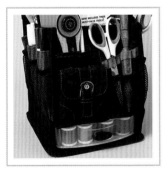

CHAPTER 5: PROJECT AND UFO STORAGE

CHAPTER 6: QUILTING ON THE GO

CHAPTER 7: LONG-TERM STORAGE AND DISPLAY

FOREWORD

The opportunity to write this book couldn't have come at a more unexpected time. I was between jobs, looking for my next career move within the marketing profession. My residential organizing business, which I established in 2004, was in full swing. My hobbies were plentiful. And the kids were at ages when homework, sports, play dates, and slumber parties filled most of the other waking hours. My calendar was completely full.

Not surprisingly, I hesitated a while before I agreed to submit a formal proposal. Excuses abounded. However, I reached a turning point when I realized that the place to start was to write down the terms for the different parts of a quilt. I titled my notebook page "Anatomy of a Quilt." That was the day I knew I would write this book.

My approach to researching this book was to spend time in many quilting studios in the Phoenix area. Without knowing me, these quilters all agreed to show me everything and anything. No holds barred.

These ladies were indispensable. I met their families, they made me lunch, we exchanged more emails, and they agreed to help in any way they could. They answered all my tough questions about their habits (good and bad), hideaways, and hang-ups. I became a student of their individual artistry as well as a problem solver for their common organizational challenges. You will see many of their brilliant ideas described here and illustrated in photos we took in their homes. Barbara even painted her studio in anticipation of the photo shoot at her house. You ladies are amazing.

I took what I learned from those great ladies and supplemented it with ideas I gathered from International Quilt Market, quilt shows, quilting stores, more quilters, podcasts, books, Web articles, blogs, magazines, and my own experience. I wrote this book to methodically guide you through the process of getting your quilting space organized. Let me take a moment to explain how to use this illustrated guide.

HOW TO USE THIS BOOK

Because Chapter 1 describes, in plain and simple steps, the process of getting organized, you need to read this chapter first. Chapter 1 will get you to look objectively at your stuff like a professional organizer does, always thinking in terms of convenience and maintainable systems. Chapter 1 will give you lots of ideas for getting organized, but you should keep reading through Chapters 2, 3, 4, and 5 before diving in. When you have gathered all the new ideas you want to try, you will definitely want to refer back to Chapter 1 to use the organizing steps from that chapter to implement the new solutions.

Chapter 2 outlines the basics of space planning and room design. As Chapter 1 explains, having an efficiently designed quilting space is fundamental to the success of your organizing efforts. You will take away from Chapter 2 design concepts behind furniture placement, furniture scale, furniture usefulness, and available storage options. Apply these space-planning concepts to create the best furniture flow through your space and to accommodate creature comforts such as lighting, heating/cooling, and ergonomics. Then you will be ready to commit to the specific organizing ideas you want to implement from Chapters 3, 4, and 5. For more detailed information about space planning in general, I recommend that you consult some of the wealth of published resources on interior design.

Some of the space-planning concepts in Chapter 2 are geared toward quilters who enjoy a whole room for their craft. But if you are the proud owner of just a quilting corner or closet, don't despair—many of the ideas will apply to you too. And there are plenty of compact storage ideas in Chapter 6 that you can adapt, along with other ideas from Chapters 3, 4, and 5.

The second section of the book, chapters 3, 4, and 5, delve into specific organizing solutions for fabric, notions, and projects, respectively. My intent with the ideas in these chapters is to inspire you to create solutions that are all your own. These chapters are full of photographs of storage ideas and organizing solutions that really work. As you read through these chapters and find an organizing solution to a problem you have, tailor it to your needs by adding your own enthusiasm, creativity, and style. Your solutions need to make you both organized and happy. If you see the perfect "thing" featured in this book, check the Author Favorites resources section (pages 107–110) for manufacturer and retail information.

If you already know what area you need organizational help with, search in Chapters 3, 4, or 5 for the appropriate section. The table of contents at the start of each chapter lists the most common quilting supplies. Try getting started with one of these trouble spots before you turn your entire quilting space on its head. You might get your feet wet first by beginning with a single problem and then practicing the steps from Chapter 1 to get and stay organized. And don't forget to refer back to Chapter 2 when considering how that solution might affect the layout of storage options in your space.

Over and over again in researching this book, I met quilters whose organizational problems weren't caused as much by the stuff as by the process of managing multiple quilting projects. If that is your issue as well, I wrote Chapter 5 for you. Whereas Chapter 3 deals exclusively with fabric and Chapter 4 deals with thread, tools, and notions, Chapter 5 is dedicated to handling, completing, and storing projects.

Chapters 6 and 7 cover topics that are still important to the overall life cycle of your quilting projects. Chapter 6 focuses on how to stay organized when you are quilting in more modest quarters or when you are away from home. Get ready to pack your quilting gear and go, because Chapter 6 will help you scale down to size while still being able to make progress on your projects when away from home.

Chapter 7 gives you practical advice on when and how to properly store and display your quilts so that they will last for generations. After all your efforts to get your supplies organized and to maintain those organizational systems, Chapter 7 is dedicated to storing your finished works. You will learn how and where to pack them away to minimize damage and handling, and how to display them around the house or at an exhibition. Your beautiful quilts deserve to be shared and preserved.

To you, members of the worldwide quilting community, I will be a lifelong admirer of your creative expression and amazing handiwork. I wish you many years of inspiration and a daily serving of tidy.

CW

section 1: get organized
(THE OVERVIEW)

ORGANIZING SOLUTIONS FOR EVERY QUILTER

THE PROCESS OF getting organized:
A STEP-BY-STEP GUIDE

This book offers a visual feast of organizing ideas, methods, and tools for your quilting space. The ideas will tickle your fancy and scintillate your senses. But, before you jump right in to find solutions to your organizational challenges, it is my duty as a professional organizer to start you off on your organizing journey by first grounding you in the fundamentals of *how* to get organized. If you feel compelled to skip ahead to later chapters to browse through the fantastic pictures of organizing solutions, be sure to come back to this chapter to understand and embrace the principles that will teach you how to get organized and, more important, *how to stay that way.*

The steps themselves are simple. But there is work involved—sometimes a lot of work. Prepare yourself to do a lot of thinking about making your space and your organizational systems more efficient. Then, know that you will be making many decisions to determine what stays, what goes, and where to put it all. Perhaps the toughest work of all will be establishing the new routines and discipline you need to stop the clutter from building up again in your newly organized space. It really will be worth it. Let's get organized.

Getting organized is the process of making things easier on yourself. You'll get more quilting done because you'll waste less time trying to find things. You'll have exactly the right tools and materials at your fingertips because they'll have a home. And you'll save money because you'll be able to keep better track of the supplies you already own.

Best of all, you get to walk into your quilting space and feel the calmness that comes when everything is in its place. Less clutter, more creativity. Less chaos, more quilting. What a great way to get your creative juices flowing.

It won't take you long to get the hang of getting and staying better organized. You'll be so motivated that you'll want to move on to get your garage and kitchen in order, followed by every other space in your life. Luckily, the steps you follow to organize your quilting space are the same ones you would use to organize a garage or a kitchen. Once your quilting space is under control, move on to lead the family charge in getting the rest of your house and life in order. Getting organized is infectious. But, since we are here to talk about your quilting stuff, let's confine our enthusiasm to your quilting space and start there.

Step 1:
Identify the Causes of the Clutter 14

Step 2:
Set Goals to Deal with the Clutter 16

Step 3:
Organize the Stuff 19

Step 4:
Maintain the Organization 26

Every organizing project, no matter the size or the place, follows the same basic steps.

Getting organized requires a plan, time and effort, and some follow-through.

STEP 1: IDENTIFY THE CAUSES OF THE CLUTTER

Identifying the things that caused the clutter in the first place is your first step in getting organized. Stand still and look objectively at your quilting space. Scrutinize the areas that clog up, and think about where your system went wrong.

You might be tempted to answer that lack of time or laziness got in the way of keeping your space neat and tidy. But I bet your problems are more likely to be rooted in inconvenience and inaccessibility than to be caused by attention deficit disorder.

CAUSES OF CLUTTER

These are common causes of clutter buildup. Do any of these sound familiar?

Not enough surface space—When you don't have enough surfaces, the piles start mounting. Piles on the floor. Piles on the chair. Piles on the piles.

The lack of shelves in this room causes piles to stack upward.

Too much surface space—Yes, you really can have enough surface area in your quilting space. And, yes, the extra empty space really does attract stray stuff.

Too many projects at once—Your work surfaces are cluttered with your current quilt as well as other well-intentioned projects, like a block-of-the-month here and a wedding gift there.

Unfinished cleanup—The remains from the last project are still floating around and taking up valuable space.

Inaccessible storage—You can't reach where something belongs, either because it's inconveniently out of reach on a top shelf or packed behind other stuff.

No designated home—You never decided where something should go, so it hasn't moved from where you originally put it.

Identifying the causes of the clutter can be the hardest step. We cut corners, we make excuses, and we procrastinate about getting organized. That happens when we encounter an obstacle that we sometimes don't even acknowledge. It may not be obvious until you're busy working in your space, and you find yourself about to take a shortcut or add to the mess. It's then that you need to stop long enough to ask yourself what the obstacle is.

If you need some help sleuthing out the problems, have someone sit with you while you work. Talk out loud while you move around the room. Narrate what you are thinking to help explain in what ways your space isn't convenient or efficient. *Those* are the causes of your clutter.

Now, move on to Step 2 in the organizing process to change the things that cause bottlenecks. Smooth, efficient systems that don't take extra effort to maintain will make you feel at ease in your quilting space, and you'll love spending time there.

STEP 2: SET GOALS TO DEAL WITH THE CLUTTER

In Step 1, you thought long and hard about why your wonderful quilting supplies tragically morphed into clutter. You figured out what caused your belongings to build up.

Clutter busting involves fixing the causes of clutter. However, the fix is almost never to go out and purchase a dozen clear plastic containers. So put your car keys back in your purse for now. You'll be staying home at least until you have a couple of sets of goals in place.

The first set of goals should solve problems and inconveniences posed by the *infrastructure* of your quilting space. The second set of goals should solve the various challenges you have in organizing your quilting *stuff*. Get started by listing what needs to be changed to eliminate the clutter and to get better organized.

> **YOUR ORGANIZING GOALS SHOULD BE BASED ON TWO THINGS:**
>
> Room characteristics to change
>
> Stuff that needs to be better organized

LIST 1: INFRASTRUCTURE CHANGES

Setting goals for creating a more efficient quilting space begins with identifying what works and what doesn't work for you in terms of infrastructure. Infrastructure refers to the fixed features of the space, such as the floor, walls, furniture, storage space, and ambience.

Make a list with two columns. On the left, write down the characteristics of your room that you like. These are the "keep" things that you will want to take advantage of and emphasize. On the right, list the things you will want to change. Room characteristics to change are often the underlying causes of the clutter.

ROOM CHARACTERISTICS TO KEEP	ROOM CHARACTERISTICS TO CHANGE
Ample room size	Poor air-conditioning in summer
Sufficient heating in winter	Ceiling fan blows items around
Easy-to-sweep wood laminate floor	Not enough drawers
Favorite paint colors on walls	Not enough shelves
Good natural light	Closet doors get in the way
Strong wireless Internet connection	Uncomfortable chair
	Design wall too small
	Lack of plants
	Folding plastic table needs to be upgraded to commercial sewing table

Looking at your own list, appreciate and emphasize the features of the space that you like and change those that you don't. The more efficient you make the room by breaking down inhibitors to your productivity, the more organized you can be.

Emphasize the things you like and change the things you don't. Making your space more functional and inviting will help you get and stay organized.

Hire a handyperson for repairs. Ask a friend with good interior design skills to help you with furniture and decorating. Replace sliding closet doors with bifold or pocket doors. Add electrical outlets. Order more functional window coverings. Within the usual constraints of time and money, start making infrastructure changes to the space that will make it easier to get organized and even more fun to quilt there.

LIST 2: ORGANIZATIONAL CHANGES

The organizational changes are different from the infrastructure changes. Whereas infrastructure changes involve the fixed features of your space, organizational changes involve the variable features, mostly about what stuff goes where.

Start by listing the big stuff, like "make more space for my stash" or "weed out unfinished projects." Then break down those big goals into smaller, more manageable tasks that keep you moving ahead without getting overwhelmed by all the work.

Having big goals broken down into little tasks is especially useful if your time is limited. If you have just a few minutes to spare, pick something that sounds like fun, get it done, and then cross it off the list. In small steps, you'll make big progress toward tackling daunting tasks.

 Give yourself a feeling of accomplishment by checking even the small things off the list.

SET A BUDGET

When assessing the list of changes that will make your quilting space more efficient and better organized, it is always important to know how much the changes will cost.

Without having seen all the great ideas in Chapters 3, 4, and 5 yet, you might find it hard to make an itemized budget, but you can start by deciding how much you have to spend. As you progress through the book and through the organizing process, prioritize your expenses against your budget and keep track of what you spend.

ESTABLISH A TIME FRAME FOR THE PROJECT

Get your quilting space organized within a reasonable time frame. Don't fall into the trap of saying you will get organized "as soon as possible." Instead, determine *actual dates*.

Look at the calendar, assess how much time you have to work on the items on your lists of infrastructure and organizational changes, and then pick dates. Set a different completion date for each major challenge, so that you have milestones along the way. Here's an example:

Set a date for completing every organizing task, and stick to it.

tip

- Sort through entire fabric stash—before school lets out for summer break

- Add more shelves to closet and get taller bookcase—before kids go back to school

- Relocate design wall—September 30

- Upgrade sewing table—Christmas

Then, be sure you focus on getting the little things done that contribute to getting the big things done, so that you can stick to your timeline.

Utilize wall space when you need more storage options.

If you fall behind or lose focus, call in the cavalry. Invite your mother-in-law, your best friend, or a bunch of quilting friends to help you. Hire a professional organizer. Do whatever you can to stick with your target dates. It is genuinely dispiriting to set great plans for getting better organized and then not follow through.

Getting organized is addictive. You will begin to see wonderful changes that make your sewing tools easier to find, and you may even dream up new project ideas using supplies you had forgotten you had.

STEP 3: ORGANIZE THE STUFF

Your goal-setting steps are complete. You have identified the causes of your quilting clutter, and you have set goals relating to what to change, where to start, how much to spend, and when to have your organization project completed. Now it's finally time to get your hands dirty and actually start organizing your stuff.

Have you noticed that I still haven't told you to go out and buy a bunch of plastic containers? Wait a little longer. It's coming.

SET UP A STAGING AREA

Before you get started, make the sorting process easier by creating a staging area. This might be a temporary table or even your cutting table and ironing board. But give yourself a place to collect each group of items as you sort through it. On the table, set out some bowls, baking trays, or even muffin tins from the kitchen to keep things separated as you sort.

Your staging area is where you should also set up your trash bin and some grocery bags for giveaways. Label each bag according to its final destination: "Give back to Mom," "Gifts for Susan," and "Donate to charity."

> **tip** *Paper grocery sacks are terrific for sorting. They stand up on their own and hold their shape—perfect for collecting stuff as you go. Write the destination for the stuff on the front of the bag in permanent marker.*

SORT

Where to Start?

Begin your sorting in a place that bothers you. Choose that tricky spot that you know will motivate you to organize more once you finally get that area whipped into shape.

EMPTY IT OUT

In your starting place of choice, take everything out. Open up the drawers and bins and baskets and bags and tins. Empty the shelves. Clear off the surfaces. This gives you a blank slate that will allow you to put everything back together in a more organized way.

ONE AREA AT A TIME

It is so easy to get off track in the sorting process. In the middle of sorting one drawer, you find things that belong in another. So you stop to sort the other and then realize that you were only halfway through the first drawer. Yikes.

Avoid rushing in and trying to organize everything at once. Instead, sort through one area or one kind of thing at a time, based on the time you have available—several pattern boxes, all rulers, the top drawer in your sewing table, every single tote bag, all batiks, whatever. Plus, focusing on one area or thing at a time gives you time to consider the best organizing solutions for your quilting habits.

As you are sorting, you are likely to find more stuff you totally forgot to put on the list of organizational changes from Step 2 (page 16). Keep that list handy and make updates to it frequently. Add stuff. Cross out other stuff.

> **tip** *Sort only one area or type of thing at a time to keep from getting overwhelmed and to inspire you to do more.*

To Keep or Not to Keep—That Is the Question

As you handle each item, decide its fate. Are you going to keep it or discard it? Even if you want to keep something, ask yourself if it needs to be improved. Is it completely functional? Sometimes we get used to our stuff and lose sight of the fact that the item is the wrong size, worn out, obsolete, not handy, or doesn't work very well any more.

HOW MUCH IS TOO MUCH?

"How much is too much?" you ask. I answer, "Too much is when you run out of space, or the cost of storing your stuff exceeds the value you get from it." That means you would get more value (more enjoyment, more pleasure) from repurposing the space currently occupied by something else.

> *tip* *When you make the decision to store something, think of its storage* value. *Make a conscious decision that the* value *you get from storing that something is worth the cost of not being able to use the space for something else. It's a trade-off.*

Stay focused by organizing one area or type of thing at a time.

CHANGE BAD ORGANIZATIONAL SOLUTIONS

As you methodically sort through your quilting space, this is your chance to change it! So add something that needs to be improved or replaced to your list of organizational goals (from Step 2 of the organizing process, page 16). Or, make a shopping list and put it with your purse and keys so that you remember to buy replacements.

Sorting through everything is your chance to admit that some item or your original organizing idea isn't working very well for you. Now is the time to make the change.

Not Keeping

Sorted items don't all have to end up back in your quilting space. Here are some ideas for helping them make an exit:

- Give them away (family, friends, charity, or freecycle.org).

- Trash them (dump them in the big trash bin outside).

- Replace them (with something newer/better/faster/prettier).

- Sell them (Craigslist.org, Etsy.com, eBay.com).

- Recycle them (either in the traditional curbside pickup sense or in the giving-them-new-life-as-something-else sense).

If you find things that don't belong in your sewing room at all, like a stray pair of socks, the missing TV remote, and last week's mail, walk them right back to where they actually belong and put them away.

Now, clear your area of the stuff to be given away, trashed, replaced, sold, or recycled, so you are left with just the items you want to keep.

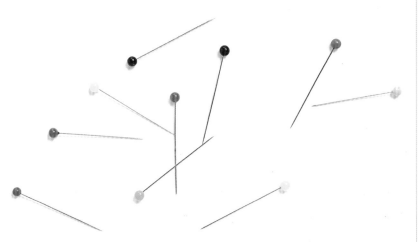

Keeping

Your staging area now contains the items you plan to keep—the things you use and love. Your core things are ready for another round of being sorted into smaller groups and measured for their new homes.

GROUP LIKE ITEMS

Put your "keep" stuff into groups of like items. Put the basting pins in a group. Place your machine needles together. For this step, use the assortment of makeshift containers you set up in your staging area (page 19) to temporarily keep the groups separated while you sort.

The grouping-like-items stage is the perfect time to further *subdivide* your supplies. Hunt down all your patterns and group them by type, size, or source. Make a different stack for each magazine title. Subdivide your embellishments into charms, beads, buttons, sequins, and others.

The better sorted your items are at the end of this stage, the more effective you will be at selecting the right method and place for storing them.

> **NOTE**
> Divide, subdivide, and subdivide again. The more you subdivide, the easier it is to select the right storage solution.

Oops.
Don't Keep Too Much!

If you are genuinely shocked by how many rotary cutters and pairs of scissors you found in the grouping process and thought you might keep, take the opportunity to weed some out. Keep the best and get rid of the rest.

You can make use of duplicates without creating excuses for hanging on to clutter: They can go into a quilting-on-the-go kit that you can keep separate for sewing sessions at friends' houses. Or, just give your duplicates away to some very appreciative new quilters.

Cutting and sewing stations

PUTTING THINGS BACK

There is a process within a process for putting things where they belong.

The first step in putting things away is deciding where the most convenient place would be for them to go. Shake it up. Be creative and open-minded. Take care to correct the original causes of your clutter (page 14).

Designate Stations

Your stuff will go back into *stations*. A station is a designated part of the room that is dedicated to a particular activity. Everything you need for that activity should be conveniently located within that station.

Most quilting spaces intuitively feature these stations:

- An ironing and pressing station
- A cutting station
- A design station
- A sewing and serging station

Some other possibilities include the following:

- A laundry station
- A computer station
- A reference library station

Preventing your newly sorted supplies from becoming ugly clutter is a matter of making it convenient to access your supplies and to maintain the organization. Stations are a great way to ensure that you have everything you need at your fingertips. Easy to take out. Easy to put away.

> **NOTE**
>
> A *station* is a smaller area within a larger space that accommodates one activity. Items associated with each activity should be colocated in that station.

Assess the Amount of Storage Space in the Station

Your job now is to assess the storage space you have available in your station. Will it accommodate all the items you want to put there so that they are convenient to get out and to put back? Get out the tape measure and begin measuring dimensions (length, width, and height) of drawers, shelves, tabletops, and so on.

Decide Which Group Fits Where

By looking at or measuring the volume of each subdivided group of items you sorted, you should have an excellent idea of how much space within the station the group will take up.

We'll revisit this in Chapter 3 as we determine storage solutions for tools and notions, but the concept of *compartmentalization* means that you keep your subdivided groups separate in their storage area.

Whether you use matching food storage containers of varying sizes or adjustable drawer trays, you will create compartments for each type of item to avoid jumbling them back into a mixed-up mess. Compartmentalizing will help you find things faster and make better use of what you already have.

For now, feel free to keep your subdivided groups in the makeshift containers that you borrowed from the kitchen. Use them to test how your groups fit into the available storage space in the station until you find the perfect containers for the final solution in the next step.

Containerize

Now you are at the putting-things-away stage, where you finally have permission to go shopping for the dozen plastic containers you've been dying to get.

STOP—BEFORE YOU SHOP

A few preliminary words of caution. Before you make any container decisions, read through Chapters 3, 4, and 5 to get helpful ideas for containerizing your quilting supplies—Chapter 3 for fabric, Chapter 4 for notions, and Chapter 5 for projects. Also, be sure to keep an eye on your budget. A new bin here and a new basket there can still add up.

Instead of spending money willy-nilly on any old containers, you've followed the process and know exactly what you're shopping for. Here's why:

- You decided which station the stuff belongs in.

- You measured the available storage space in the station.

- You know how long, wide, and deep each shelf or drawer or surface is.

- You know how big your groups of sorted stuff are.

KNOW YOUR MEASUREMENTS

Now, through the power of elementary school math (length × width × height), you can go shopping—tape measure and list of space dimensions in hand—to find a perfectly sized bin, bag, basket, or box that will hold the stuff within the storage space available. Containers can be purchased or repurposed household objects—whichever suits your taste and budget. Voilà! You are that much closer to organizational nirvana.

Here's an example:

You have a library station with five shelves. Each shelf is 14″ high, 20″ long, and 12″ deep.

You are matching that 14″h × 20″l × 12″d shelf space to a group of magazines you sorted that is subdivided into five stacks of different titles. Each stack is 12″ tall.

The containers you have selected (because you read Chapter 3) are magazine holders.

Now you are shopping for ten magazine holders that are 6″ wide (two holders for each title), less than 14″ high (to fit within the height of each shelf), and no more than 12″ deep (to fit the depth of each shelf).

Always have your measurements with you when you go shopping. You never know where you're going to run across the perfect solution. Having your measurements with you will guarantee that what you buy will fit in your space.

tip

Put Everything in a Designated Home

It's the last step in the putting-things-away process: put everything in its new home. When something has a home, you'll know where to find it the next time you need it, which also means you always need to put it back where it belongs.

Keep in mind, as you put everything in its new place, that your new organizing solutions should be not only convenient but also pleasing to the eye. Attractive and convenient is the winning combination for getting and staying organized. The prettier your space looks, the more motivated you will be to keep it organized.

As you find a home for everything, avoid wasting space. In each station, work within your storage space dimensions, taking the time to readjust shelves, move around drawers, and change configurations to make sure you can fit everything comfortably and conveniently into the space you have. This is how you keep it organized, because it's quick and easy to maintain.

> Attractive and convenient is the winning combination for getting and staying organized.

Use storage accessories, like this under-shelf basket, to recapture space that would otherwise go unused.

STEP 4: MAINTAIN THE ORGANIZATION

You have your furniture and quilting supplies all conveniently placed and beautifully arranged. You have designated homes for everything, and now putting stuff away is a snap! You feel energized every time you walk into the room. Gone is that sense of overwhelm and that unsettled feeling that you don't have control over your own stuff.

Still, your organizing work isn't quite over. Now your job becomes keeping your space tidy, every day.

DAILY MAINTENANCE

Maintaining your new organizational systems involves commitment and discipline. Mainly, you will need to change your daily habits and set new rules for yourself.

Set New Rules

When you set a new rule for yourself, say it out loud to someone else. Tell a family member or a quilting friend what you are going to do to keep yourself organized.

Resolve to tidy up your work space at the end of each work session and to completely clean up your work space at the completion of each project. Put scraps away based on size. Return tools to their designated homes. Place leftover yardage back in the stash. Resolve to never have fabric and rulers out that you aren't actively using.

If you routinely have multiple projects going at once, resolve to tidy up one before moving on to another. Chapter 5 offers ideas for keeping individual projects contained and separated. Tidying up one project frees up valuable work space for another. You get a fresh perspective and a clean start.

But if you're a habitual nonfinisher, set a new maximum number of unfinished projects that you can keep at a time, so that you don't hang on to projects you will never complete.

FINDING HOMES FOR NEW TREASURES

After you have been shopping or quilting away from home, the very first thing to do when you return home is put away your new purchases and unpack your bags. All that fun travel and shopping requires some tedious follow-up. Put everything away immediately. Most plastic shopping bags aren't even transparent, so it is surprisingly easy to forget what's inside. No stray bags with who-knows-what inside.

Maintaining your new organizational systems involves commitment and discipline.

> *After you have been shopping or quilting away from home, the very first thing to do when you return home is put away your new purchases and unpack your bags.*

tip

When you come home from a class with a charming half-finished project, decide quickly whether you will realistically finish it and whether it ranks high enough to keep within your new maximum number of unfinished projects. It's okay to let it go when you know it served the purpose of teaching you the technique. You don't have to finish it. But if you keep it, make notes about what you were practicing and where you left off.

Buying only what you need or to replace what you have used goes a long way toward keeping clutter at bay.

STOP ATTRACTING STRAY STUFF

To keep yourself organized, you also need to keep your stuff under control. Say no if someone offers you supplies you don't need. Resist buying new gadgets if you don't have a problem that needs to be solved. More stuff requires more space—space you probably don't have. Purposeful shopping to buy only what you need or to replace what you have used also goes a long way in keeping clutter at bay.

THE GIFT OF GIVING

On a regular basis, take a few minutes to go through one kind of item, such as your patterns or your rotary cutters, and keep just your favorites. Give away the rest. Generously gifting to others, especially to new quilters, is an excellent way to keep and store just what you use and love. In the process, you are helping someone else love quilting as much as you do.

USE WHAT YOU ALREADY HAVE

Most quilters have an abundance of fabric. Make that an overabundance. And you know who you are. Use what you already have in your stash. You will save money, save time, and gradually whittle down your fabric stash to a more manageable quantity. If you keep passing over some questionable fabrics, package them up and give them away. Use your storage space for the fabrics you know you are going to use.

Repurposed food containers make ideal gift packages for friends.

Use what you already have in your stash. You will save money, save time, and gradually whittle down your fabric stash to a more manageable quantity.

ORGANIZING SOLUTIONS FOR EVERY QUILTER

room design

ROOM DESIGN BASICS

The basic design of your room refers to the orientation of the room and the placement of furniture and other items within it. Most room design is determined by the room's wall/window/door configuration and, even if only subconsciously, by the furniture pieces you have in the room.

When professionals redesign a room, they remove *everything*, until the room is just four walls and a floor. They do this so they can work with a clean slate, bringing back in the largest furniture items first and placing them where they are both the most functional and the most aesthetically pleasing.

STARTING FROM SCRATCH

To breathe new life into a stale quilting space, question everything. If you have the gumption to actually remove everything from your quilting room and then build the room back up from scratch, do it.

If just the idea of moving piles of stuff and heavy furniture into other rooms of your house makes you weak in the knees, you might take the easier way out and spend a few focused minutes thinking hard about how you actually use your room. Get a second opinion if you need to. Talk over your observations and ideas with a friend.

You have probably been quilting in there for a while already, so you know how often you have to get up from your chair to retrieve something out of your reach. Although you don't always consciously think of it, it may really bother you that your scrap bin isn't close enough for you to toss scraps into without standing up from your sewing table. And maybe you have just resigned yourself to the fact that you have to do your hand quilting projects in the breakfast nook so you have enough natural light to see all those delicate stitches.

If your processes, habits, preferences, and stuff have changed since you first arranged your room, it may be high time for a change. But don't change for change's sake. Rather, change for greater efficiency and ease of use—and so you absolutely, positively love the areas where you quilt.

ASSESSING FURNITURE NEEDS

After thinking long and hard about how well your existing room design works for you today and even sharing those thoughts with a friend, you can begin any redesign by assessing how well your furniture is performing for your needs.

Refer back to Chapter 1 for the work you have already done in assessing the positive and negative infrastructure features of your quilting space (page 16). You don't have to know yet *where* your furniture will be placed in the room. You just need to determine *whether* it is staying and what you would replace it with if you needed to. Thinking through the grand plan for furniture will give you the work and storage infrastructure you need to go merrily on your way.

JUDGE YOUR CURRENT FURNITURE

Study each piece of furniture in your room and ask yourself objectively how well each one serves its intended purpose. How could your furniture serve you better?

> ### THE FOUR MOST IMPORTANT FEATURES FOR QUILTING FURNITURE:
>
> Surface area   Scale
>
> Height   Storage

Surface Area

You need enough surface area—but not too much—primarily for your cutting table and for your machine table. Some quilters like additional surface area to stage projects, especially for piecing, and to have free space for when friends come over to quilt.

Height

For work surfaces, you will need to focus on two heights. One will be for your sewing surface and the other for your cutting surface.

SEWING SURFACE HEIGHT

To know the ideal heights for you, begin by sitting in your sewing chair. Be sure that your chair is set at a height so that your feet are flat on the floor. With your arms at your sides and elbows bent so that your forearms are at 90° from your upper arms, measure from your elbow to the floor. Add 5½"–7" to that measurement to calculate the final sewing table height, which is usually between 28" and 36" (71–91cm).

CUTTING TABLE HEIGHT

Your cutting surface should be quite a bit higher than your sewing table. To determine the best height for you, stand with your feet flat on the floor and your arms straight forward and bent 90° at the elbow. Your forearms should lie flat on the cutting table. This height is likely to be between 36" and 40" (91–102cm).

Adapt the height of your cutting table so that your forearms lay flat on the surface when you stand.

Scale

The scale of your furniture needs to be proportional both to the room and to its purpose in your quilting process. Again, put on your Goldilocks attitude and judge your furniture based on whether it is too big, too small, or just right for where it is and how you use it.

Storage

After surface area, height, and scale, storage is the fourth most important criterion for judging furniture in a quilting space. Storage refers to the *versatility* and *volume* of available drawers, cubbies, shelves, and cupboards.

CONSIDERING NEW FURNITURE

Running out and buying all new furniture for your quilting space is rarely an option. But with this fresh perspective on comfort and versatility, you might be considering budgeting and shopping for new furniture items with improved features.

I have to say that as a professional organizer, I was prepared to be wowed by the ready-made sewing tables from the big-name manufacturers. But I haven't been. I thought the array of drawers and cubbies would dazzle me, but I realized that their expensive storage options are just as prone to being as badly organized as a $40 plastic drawer unit from a discount retailer.

Mind you, some of the features of fancy sewing tables, such as height-adjustable pneumatic legs, lockable casters, drop leaves, and machine airlifts justify their fancy prices. If you have $3,000 to spend on a top-of-the-line sewing table, by all means, spend away.

But the reality is that no one sewing table could possibly fit everyone's needs. The perfect sewing table is one that suits your quilting style and allows you to work comfortably and efficiently within the space you have. If you have something you love, keep it. If you don't love it, replace it. Whatever you have, keep it organized well.

Whatever you are now looking for, your shopping radar should be up while browsing thrift stores, garage sales, online classifieds, consignment furniture shops, or even curbside discards. Keep your space measurements handy because you might be surprised to find the perfect solutions in the most unlikely places.

> The perfect sewing table is one that suits your quilting style and allows you to work comfortably and efficiently within the space you have.

FURNITURE PLACEMENT

Now that you have studied your furniture pieces from every angle, having evaluated them for every imaginable feature and use, the next step in room design is to place the pieces.

PLACE THE MOST IMPORTANT FURNITURE FIRST

If you have cleared out the entire room for this step, my hat's off to you. You can start bringing back the furniture pieces, one at a time, starting with the largest, most important items. That probably means you'll be kicking off the arrangement with your sewing table, longarm, quilting frame, or cutting table.

Nancy Arseneault stores her stash inside a free-standing closet system. She covered the closet doors with felt to serve as design walls.

Photo by Nancy Arseneault

Don't know where to put it? Stand in the doorway or in a corner and stare at the room for a while. Perhaps the sewing table should face a window so that you can enjoy the view outside. Alternatively, you might prefer to have the table angled toward the door, so that you can see into other parts of the house. The placement of the sewing table may even be restricted by the location of electrical outlets in the room. In the end, be sure to give your most important furniture the prime real estate it deserves. Figure out where it goes first and then accommodate the rest of the furniture around it.

FLOW AND BALANCE

Your furniture arrangement will influence the flow around the room. *Flow* refers to how you move around and navigate through your room. Place the furniture to optimize the flow through the room.

For balance, make sure that your room isn't more heavily weighted on one side than on the other, meaning that the height and bulk of the furniture and belongings seem unevenly distributed. Also be sure not to push everything up against the walls, leaving a big dead space in the center of the room.

You might be interested, at this point, in calling upon a friend with interior design skills or even in employing the principles of the Chinese art of *feng shui*. Feng shui is believed to improve the flow of life energy through the home by harmonizing the placement or orientation of items with the natural environment.

CLUSTER FURNITURE INTO STATIONS

As you place each item, keep in mind the principle of creating *stations* (pages 22–23). A station refers to a compact area in which you have all the furniture and supplies you need for a certain activity.

The most obvious stations in a quilting space include the following:

- An ironing and pressing station
- A cutting station
- A piecing and design station
- A sewing and serging station

Thinking in terms of stations will help you arrange your furniture, storage items, and supplies so they are conveniently located together and avoid causing clutter.

Ironing and Pressing Station

The centerpiece of your ironing and pressing station will be your ironing board—or the ironing pad atop a table surface. In keeping with the concept of having all your tools conveniently located in the station, you will no doubt also have your iron, mini iron, finger-pressing tools, pressing sheets, and any starch or finishing sprays you use.

Cutting Station

A cutting station is very straightforward in its contents. Front and center is the cutting surface. Be sure your cutting surface is the correct ergonomic height (page 30). In addition to the surface, you will need to have your plethora of cutting tools within easy reach. Your everyday rotary cutter, utility scissors, and thread scissors might hang on the wall. Other lesser-used implements, such as fabric shears, appliqué scissors, pinking shears, embroidery shears, buttonhole scissors, or bent-handle dressmaking shears can be safely tucked away on rubberized shelf liner in a shallow drawer.

A SAMPLE INVENTORY FOR YOUR PRESSING STATION:

- Iron
- Stabilizers
- Iron cleaner (Coarse salt on butcher paper works best for steel-plate irons.)
- Mini iron
- Appliqué iron
- Spray starch
- EZE-View cotton pressing cloth
- Spray sizing
- Teflon pressing sheet
- For dressmakers: sleeve board, tailor's board, pressing ham, Ezy-Hem gauge, hem clips
- Spray bottle for distilled water
- Sewing gauge

Piecing and Designing Station

Key to a successful design station is enough wall and table surface to match the size of your most common projects. Your design wall should be large enough to provide perspective on your color and pattern choices. Cover just about any surface in flannel or batting to magically transform it into a designing surface. You might make use of a handy stash of pins, clips, sticky notes, and a pencil at this station for hanging heavier items and for jotting down thoughts.

Sewing and Serging Station

The hub of a quilting space is the sewing and serging station. Machine quilters and longarm quilters place their machines at the center. Hand quilters have their quilting frames or sewing surfaces as the focus. Although it is tempting to locate just about every other item related to quiltmaking in this station, work on keeping it simple. In Chapter 1, we discussed grouping and subdividing supplies (page 21). Keep your table surfaces clear by including just the must-haves, and storing lesser-used items farther and farther from the sewing table.

Additional Stations

As you continue to evaluate the placement of furniture and items in your quilting space, there are a few additional stations that you should consider in your design plans:

• A laundry station

• A computer station

• A reference library station

Here are some organizational and containerizing tips for each one.

LAUNDRY STATION

Although the laundry station is usually located somewhere else in the house, I have yet to meet a quilter who doesn't have a laundry station stocked with assorted washing products that rival those of a well-intentioned new mother, whose nesting exploits have led to an assemblage of boxes and jugs labeled "hypoallergenic," "fragrance free," or "gentle on baby's skin."

A quilter's laundry room might feature, among other products, Orvus WA Paste, quilt soap, fabric dyes, Synthrapol (for removing excess dye), Retayne (a color fixative for commercially dyed fabrics), vinegar (for removing some stains, odors, and residues), and Shout Color Catchers (for trapping loose dyes in wash water).

Be sure to group these items together as well as possible so that they are within easy reach from your washer, dryer, and laundry sink. Find the right product at your fingertips by using lazy Susan turntables or tall plastic baskets that fit your laundry cabinet shelves.

Laundry station supplies are grouped on a turntable.

COMPUTER STATION

Another overlooked quilting station is the computer station. For all of you Electric Quilt users, email addicts, bloggers, and iTunes fanatics, having your computer set up in your quilting studio is a must. Along with your computer, this station will include a monitor, a keyboard, a mouse, plain paper, software CDs, user manuals, a printer, ink cartridges, inkjet fabric sheets, and even freezer paper (for transfers and templates).

Depending upon your room configuration, a computer station will probably necessitate a desk and chair in addition to the ones used in your sewing station. Keep this station free of projects and stray fabric bundles by minimizing the desk size and respecting the boundaries between stations.

You may have no choice about mingling quilting projects with office supplies if your quilting computer is also your online bill-pay computer, the kids' homework computer, or the family gaming computer.

REFERENCE LIBRARY STATION

The last oft-overlooked station is the reference library. A reference library station is usually best served by a shelving unit. Still, I have seen a charming collection of pattern books stored inside apple crates.

For those of you quilting inside what used to be just a bedroom, the top shelf of the closet is a great place for books and magazines. My best advice to you for reference materials is to *think vertically*. Go tall with bookcases, mount floating shelves to the wall, and install upper cabinets. The vertical space in a room with an average eight-foot ceiling is far too valuable to waste.

In addition to books and magazines, include your computer hardware and software user manuals, blank and labeled CDs, three-ring binders, color journals, and quilt journals. You might also include your boxes of patterns here.

GOING BEYOND ROOM DESIGN BASICS

By this point in the chapter, you are probably at one with the attributes of your room, in love with your new furniture arrangement, and amazed by the convenience of your various stations. These are the basics of a functional and organized quilting space. But you need to go beyond the basics to really say, "Good-bye, tired décor. Hello, inviting new space."

How much you love your quilting space can be heavily influenced by the aesthetics of the room. As your excitement for schlepping around furniture and toting out boxes of fabric builds, let's spend a moment assessing whether your quilting area is as snazzy as you need it to be.

COLOR AND LIGHT

The color of the walls and the amount of natural light in the room can set the mood. Can your ideal quilting sanctuary be as purple as the day is long? Oh, yes! Just keep in mind that color on the walls of a quilting space could cast that color onto everything you create. Choose the wall color carefully.

Although sunlight is no friend to your fabrics and threads, you can never have enough light in a room for quilting's detailed stitching and subtle color-matching tasks. Even if you have an unpleasant view out the window, you might want to block the view without blocking the light. A strategically planted shrub outside or a sheer curtain or textured window film inside can do the trick.

What you can't solve with sunlight, you may have to solve with electric lights.

Three Sources of Light

We have already talked about the value of natural light in the room. Because I can pretty much guarantee that you will be quilting some days before dawn and often well after dark, you will need additional artificial lighting.

> ### THERE ARE THREE SOURCES OF LIGHTING IN A ROOM:
> Ambient—brightest lighting sources
>
> Task—enhances lighting for a specific area
>
> Accent—creates mood

AMBIENT LIGHTING

A room's main source of artificial lighting is called *ambient* light. Ambient lighting is usually the brightest lighting source in the room. Most often it comes from overhead light fixtures such as a lighted ceiling fan, a series of recessed ceiling lights, or a single ceiling lamp. Since quilting engenders certain levels of obsessiveness anyway, you might even consider installing *true-color* (also called *full-spectrum*) light fixtures or bulbs for easier color matching. Don't forget to ensure that you have sufficient ambient light inside closets and cupboards.

Task lights cast light directly onto your projects.

TASK LIGHTING

The next most important source of light in your studio will come from *task* lighting. Task lighting is usually located directly over your work area. It can come from a floor lamp that directs light downward, from a spotlight directed downward from a wall or ceiling, or even from a table lamp. The most popular task lighting for quilters is a true-color light. Other useful task lights are ones underneath cabinets that shine onto countertops below and ones built into sewing machines.

OttLite for true color

ACCENT LIGHTING

The final artificial light sources that have the power to transform your sewing room from bland to beautiful are *accent* lights. Accent lighting serves to create mood in a room and can be a single light that illuminates just one décor item, such as a piece of wall art, or a track lighting fixture that illuminates a whole wall. Use accent lighting to brighten a dark corner, to draw attention to your quilt displays, or to create ambience when the room's main light is off.

TEMPERATURE

A studio with too little cooling in the summer and too little heating in the winter can feel more like a prison than a sanctuary. Make friends with your local HVAC professional, buy the most energy-efficient space heater and portable air conditioner you can afford, or opt for a different space altogether. Get on your Goldilocks attitude: not too hot, not too cold—just right for quilting bliss.

ELECTRICAL SYSTEM

Of course, being able to add heating and cooling equipment may depend on your electrical wiring. Following an electrician's counsel, be sure that you have the juice to connect all your electrical necessities, not the least of which are your iron and your sewing machine.

The number of outlets, as well as their locations, can significantly impact your positioning choices for key pieces of furniture and equipment. Wall sockets for cable television and Internet connectivity could also be factors.

> Work with an electrician to overcome cabling and wiring challenges before settling for any awkward or inconvenient room designs.

SOUND

Just like color and light, sound can make or break a room. If you are distracted by sounds (of course, you love your kids and your pets as much as your quilts!), you need to take action to stifle the ruckus. White-noise machines, a whirring fan, your own fave tunes blaring, or the gentle trickle of an indoor water feature all have the potential to get your concentration and focus back on track.

CREATURE COMFORTS

Get an adjustable ergonomic chair that fits your body dimensions to avoid strain on your back, legs, arms, wrists, and hands. Look for adjustable height, adjustable tilt, caster wheels, adjustable lumbar support, and adjustable-height armrests.

Is your floor well cushioned enough to spare your knees and back at the cutting table? An industrial antifatigue floor mat might be in order. Spice it up by covering it with a pretty floor mat that complements your décor.

A funky rug hides an industrial antifatigue mat to make standing for long periods easier on your feet.

Those are comforts for your body, but your mind may need some too. For myself, I might choose a flat-screen TV, an MP3-player sound system, a coffeemaker, and a mini fridge.

FINAL TOUCHES

I believe it is true that a house is finally a home when the pictures are up on the walls. It seems logical that we don't hang art on the walls until after we paint, after we arrange the furniture, and after we store our belongings. Only then can the final touches be addressed. Plants to soften the edges. Quilts to adorn the walls. Accent lighting to warm up the room. Rugs to brighten the floor. Accessories to add whimsy and charm.

Surrounded by the things we love in a space where we love to be, we really mean it when we say, "Good-bye, tired décor. Hello, inviting new space."

STUDIO COLOR WHEEL

section 2: storage options
(THE NITTY-GRITTY)

ORGANIZING SOLUTIONS FOR EVERY QUILTER

fabric storage

FOR THE LOVE OF FABRIC

It is the color, the pattern, the touch, the visual pleasure. The way it evokes in you a memory of someone or somewhere meaningful. You quilt to be able to express yourself, to share part of yourself with people you care about. Quilting is a shameless, unremitting love affair with fabric.

Sometimes you find the fabric, and sometimes the fabric finds you. It was just meant to be. Some of the time, you see the perfect fabric for a project you have had in mind. And other times, you realize that the fabric is so stunning that you need to find the perfect project for it. Either way, you quilt for the love of fabric.

I have met quilters who acquire and use fabric in every imaginable way. Some quilt with the fabric down to the very tiniest of scraps. Some quilt with the fabric just once and then give away the remainders. Some happy recipients of such gifts of fabric quilt almost exclusively using the scraps of others. Somehow you acquire what you need and transform it into a work of art.

ODE TO A STASH

I love you, my elegant stash;
you're dearer than
all the world's cash.

I love to just
hold you
and
fondle and fold you
and praise your
distinctive panache!

—*Author, Bill McDonald*

STORING YARDAGE

For those of you with well-rounded stashes, you have the convenience of having almost every imaginable color and pattern choice conveniently on hand. The drawback is that you probably also have way more fabric than you currently have plans for. Getting organized will involve a balance between having what you want and finding what you need.

HOW MUCH IS TOO MUCH?

In Chapter 2, I said that too much is when you run out of space or when the "cost" of storing your stuff exceeds the "value" you get from it. As an organizer, I spend lots of time teaching my clients how to live within their storage means. When your storage space runs out, your collection needs to stop.

Whether you have outgrown your space and need to whittle down your stash or whether you just want to simplify your quilting systems, one rule of thumb applies to your fabric: keep what you love; remove what doesn't excite you.

Keep what you love; remove what doesn't excite you.

Don't keep fabric if the fiber content or quality is questionable. Your space is too valuable to store junk.

Remove what doesn't excite you, even if you think "it might be useful one day." Let it be immediately useful to someone else and reward yourself with an uncluttered stash that truly fits into your studio's storage capacity.

Using your existing stash to its best advantage means keeping your fabrics *visible*. I have seen just about every method for storing fabric. And the results are sometimes meticulous and at other times ridiculous. If it works for you, stick with it. But if you are still looking for fabric storage nirvana, my favorite storage solution for fabric yardage is … drumroll, please … wire mesh baskets.

WIRE MESH BASKETS

Wire mesh baskets have the distinct advantages of being exceptionally sturdy and of breathing well, allowing air to flow freely through your fabrics.

Wire mesh baskets are usually fully removable drawers that fit into a steel frame. The baskets come in single, double, and triple depths, corresponding to how many runners they fit in between within the frame.

Another reason I recommend storing fabric yardage in wire mesh baskets is that they allow you to easily flip through your beautiful yardage: with the fabric neatly folded and set in the basket from front to back, you will see the thin, finished edges of folded fabric. This eliminates the inevitable leaning and falling problems that arise when you pull out a fabric from the middle, or worse, from the bottom, of your vertically stacked pile on a closet shelf.

Most wire mesh basket frames have the added advantage of being able to accommodate surfaces on top. Stand multiple frames together, add a tabletop, get the right ergonomic height, and you have a cutting table! Get creative with organizational solutions that serve multiple uses.

This wire mesh drawer system accommodates a tabletop surface to use as a cutting table.

Photo by Nancy Arseneault

Photo by Alex Anderson

Alex Anderson describes why she chose a wire mesh drawer system to organize her stash:

I originally kept my stash on open metal shelves, but I needed a better solution because my collection was overrunning me, and I couldn't cope with the visual mess. When I was at a home improvement store many years ago, I found this modular wire drawer and frame system that would fit in the closet of the bedroom studio. I knew it would be a terrific way to organize my stash because I could store fabric much more efficiently and could easily access my fabric. But because the system was rather costly, I had to gradually "collect" the pieces over time.

When I needed to add a third bay of drawers to accommodate my rapidly expanding stash, the sliding doors on the closet had to come off. In their place, I made curtains and hung them from a bathroom curtain tension rod to shelter the fabric from light.

With this system, you can choose baskets that are one, two, or three rungs deep. I prefer drawers that are two rungs deep because they can hold a nice amount of fabric without becoming as heavy as the three-rung drawers when they are full.

The baskets are a great solution for me because I can take them out of the closet, move them to where I am working, and then slide them quickly back into place when I am finished with that color or group of fabrics.

Alex Anderson's fabric stash is easily accessible in double-depth wire mesh baskets.

Photo by Alex Anderson

SHELVES

Boxes and Baskets

IF YOUR STASH CALLS A SHELF HOME

—Any shelf, anywhere—your challenge is to keep each vertical stack of fabric from toppling over sideways. Luckily, you have a multitude of options for keeping your stacked stash steady. Get started by selecting **boxes** with flat corners and edges that are the same depth as your shelf. You will be placing them open-end forward on the shelf so the finished edges of your folded fabric face outward and are held in place on five sides.

Looking around the home organization sections in your favorite discount retail shops, you are sure to find plastic cubes, canvas cubes, sweater boxes, or even cardboard boxes that are a comfortable width and depth so you can refold all your fabric to fit. Never waste space.

For fabric folding tips, see page 50.

If you are both blessed and cursed with extra-deep shelves, boxes turned open-end forward might be an ideal solution for accessing your stash at the back. If you layer the boxes two deep on a shelf, you can easily take out the box in front to reveal the box behind.

Baskets with colorful cotton liners can be equally useful, with the added benefit of cuteness. They probably won't stack well, but you might find that baskets of fabric groupings lined up along your shelves are so pretty that you will *want* to keep them organized. Add creative flair to labels for each container, like using scraps to indicate the color or fiber of that group.

Shelf Dividers

Shelf dividers are handy inventions for keeping all kinds of stuff from toppling over on shelves. They are most often available in vinyl-coated steel or clear acrylic. They clip onto the shelf and then stand upright to keep tall stacks in check.

Shelf dividers can also serve to visually break up your stash into smaller sections, so your mind can better process what it sees. Refer back to this concept of *compartmentalization*, or subdividing (page 23).

Shelf dividers keep tall stacks in check.

Optimize usage of your shelf height by stacking multiple bins that store fabric by color or type.

Lidded Plastic Bins

Although I am not normally an advocate of hiding things in bins, I have seen quilters (albeit quilters with admirably humble stashes) effectively store their fabric in lidded storage boxes made of clear plastic. Boxes should probably be 7–18 quarts in size, but shop for a size that optimizes usage of the width, depth, and height of your shelves or readjust your shelves to fit your boxes. Now you know why you took all those measurements in Chapters 1 and 2.

The boxes should be as *transparent* as possible because you will *remember* what you have when you can *see* your stash. The lids allow for stacking, but be aware that airtight plastic can put your fabric at risk of mildew damage. If your storage area has good airflow and is not susceptible to humidity, lidded plastic bins can be an effective means for controlling stash creep, because you can limit yourself to one bin per color or fiber group. And it's good to have limits, right?

> If it doesn't fit in the bin, it can't go into the stash!

 Label your containers, especially ones made of opaque materials such as canvas, leather, wicker, or metal.

Buy containers that optimize usage of the width, depth, and height of your shelves. But be aware that containers that are too big for the items being stored inside inevitably attract stray stuff.

HANGING CLOTHES STACKERS

If you are quilting in a space with extremely restricted storage, you could borrow storage ideas from other parts of the house. Try storing your small fabric stash in a clothes stacker that hangs from a closet rod. A clothes stacker features multiple compartments that can keep your colors or fabric types separated. It is important that the clothes stacker you use be adequately reinforced at the top so that it can hold the weight of your fabric.

In a clothes stacker, fabric will stack vertically in one or two columns per compartment. Look for a portable clothing rack on caster wheels or a decorative towel rail to implement this vertical storage solution without a closet rod.

You'll find lots of uses for a stacker in a compact vertical space. Use the different compartments to store current projects or to collect materials for planned projects. Chapter 5 will discuss even more options for keeping projects organized.

BOOKCASES

Remember in Chapter 2 when we were talking about taking advantage of vertical space (page 34)? A bookcase or tall utility cabinet will do just that. It will use a small amount of floor space while providing a large amount of storage volume.

Refer to the prior section on fabric storage ideas for shelves for ideas on storing fabric on shelves in a bookcase or cabinet. You can use the shelves of the bookcase or cabinet to store your folded fabric vertically, separated by shelf dividers, if your shelves are deep enough. Or, store fabric horizontally by placing it from back to front in a basket with the folded edges facing upward.

Note that with bookcases and other storage furniture, *you get what you pay for.* The cheap stuff is rarely versatile. A bigger budget buys you more height, more durability, more stability, and more shelves. Those shelves will also be deeper and fully adjustable. In the long run, fully adjustable shelves offer you extraordinary flexibility in designing and later reworking your quilting space as you accommodate changes to your supplies over time.

A clothes stacker can store a variety of items in a compact vertical space.

SORTING FABRIC

I bet you thought I would tell you to store all your fabric by color. You'd be wrong—at least partly wrong, anyway. In my experience, there are three or four more sort orders for yardage in your stash. And sorting by color doesn't even come first.

SORTING MATCHING SETS

The first sort order is sorting by *matching sets*. Matching sets are the fabrics you bought together because they are from the same collection or because they are set aside for the same project. You should keep matching sets together. You can store matching sets together in separate bins so you have all the pieces for a project in a single place. Or, tie them into bundles with ribbons. Or, store them together in wire mesh drawers.

Sort fabric in matching sets.

SORTING THEME FABRIC

The second sort order for yardage in your stash is for *theme fabric*. Theme fabrics are often very colorful and are difficult to classify among your regular stash. Examples of theme fabrics are holidays, kids, animals, vintage, toile, tropical, or whatever other themes catch your fancy. Further sort each theme into like colors or into fabrics of similar color value, from lightest to darkest.

You can store theme fabrics in their own wire mesh drawers or in clear, lidded plastic containers by theme, depending upon your volumes.

Group theme fabrics together.

SORTING THE CORE

The third sort order is for the bulk of your stash. These are the fabrics that are available for the taking. Your core stash is best stored in wire mesh drawers and sorted *by color.*

Sorting by color makes it readily apparent from the quantities which colors you favor and which colors you need to acquire to better rebalance the versatility of your stash. Within your core stash, it can also be a challenging and rewarding exercise to further sort your fabrics by *intensity* and *value* within the same hue: light bright reds to dark bright reds and then light dull reds to dark dull reds.

Sort the core stash by color.

SORTING THE FANCIES

Textile artists may want to employ a further round of sort orders to group together different fabrics, well above and beyond typical cottons. Hand-dyes, wools, silks, organzas, tulles, velvets, metallics, pleathers, vinyls, burlaps, and every other imaginable textile all beg to be sorted into like groups. Then sort each group by color, value, or intensity. Dedicate even more wire mesh drawers to contain them all.

Prewash fabric to ensure colorfastness, allow for shrinkage, and remove chemical allergens. If you don't prewash, at least check for colorfastness.

FOLDING FABRIC

As with any other household organizing project, the storage solution should be the same size as the items being stored. Too small won't hold everything, and too large will attract stray stuff. So you need to learn into which dimensions you need to fold your fabric.

I have looked at all manner and means of folding fabric pieces into like-sized bundles to match their containers, and the most convenient seems to be folding fabric around a ruler or a custom-cut piece of cardboard that is slightly smaller than the dimensions of the drawer, bin, or shelf. If you have the right size of ruler, try folding the fabric around the ruler, being sure the length of the new bundle is just shorter than the width of the drawer. Slide the ruler out from the middle of the newly folded bundle, and voilà!

View an online video demonstrating fabric folding around rulers. Query YouTube for "fabric folding."

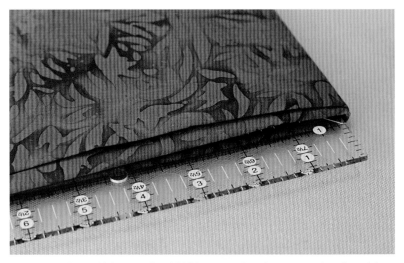

For consistently sized fabric bundles, fold fabric around a ruler or piece of cardboard that is slightly shorter in length and width than your drawer or bin.

If the mere thought of refolding all your fabric around a ruler gives you heartburn, you likely have another one of those well-endowed fabric stashes. Embrace the folding as another golden opportunity to whittle down your stash into a manageable size. As you fold, set aside the fabrics that don't inspire you anymore or that are outside your fave color palette du jour. You'll be left chomping at the bit to start sewing with your rediscovered pretties.

Still not sold on the idea of refolding? Of course, it's just fine not having everything perfectly folded, as long as you can find what you need.

MANAGING YOUR STASH

Your fabric stash is your inventory. Dig in to find great fabrics for your blocks, backing, or binding.

SEARCH YOUR STASH

First, your stash should be a convenient source for color matching and for fabrics that will work well together in the projects you have in mind.

To extend your stash's selection, try overdyeing fabrics to alter their color or turning over fabrics to reveal a lighter shade. Try swapping fabric with a friend in exchange for the color tones you need. If you can't get what you need, you might want to hustle off to the quilt shop to buy fabrics that enable you to use the ones you already own.

CHANGE YOUR FABRIC SHOPPING HABITS

If your stash never quite seems to be up to snuff, you may need to change your thinking about fabric shopping. Perhaps your stash has in it an abundance of your very favorite colors and patterns but not the additional colors and patterns you need in order to actually quilt with them. In this case, your stash may be in need of some additional flexibility.

tip

Pack swatches of fabrics you already have for a particular project into a mini photo book or into a Ziploc snack bag inside your purse for quick matching on shopping trips.

Search your stash first for the right fabrics. Then buy only the fabrics you need to complete the project.

SCRAPS, STRIPS, STRINGS, AND SELVAGES

Now that your fabric yardage is laid out in obsessively tidy rows by project, by theme, by color, and by fancy fabric type on or in your fabric storage system of choice, it's time to sweat the small stuff. Small stuff consists of scraps, strips, strings, and even selvages.

SCRAPS

You don't have to be a scrappy quilter or an appliqué addict to value holding on to your scraps. Scraps hold promise for creating even more works of art. More to the point, if the big pieces of those fabulous fabrics worked well the first time, the leftovers sure can't hurt.

But keeping scraps can become burdensome in light of the storage problems and disorganization that ensue. I've seen more than my fair share of quilters' scraps overflowing in their oversize plastic tubs underneath the cutting table. Collecting scraps is a lot like eating: everything in moderation.

Cut into Predetermined Sizes

Joan Ford, creator of ScrapTherapy cutting workshops and quilt designs, tells a great story about when she recognized that her scrap-saving habits were getting the best of her. "I realized I was saving these scraps for someone else to inherit when I'm dead," she quips. With no end in sight to her deposits into the scrap heap, Joan decided to make her scraps work for her. She began cutting them down into standard sizes and then storing each size in a separate plastic shoe bin.

Offered exclusively through quilt shops, Joan's ScrapTherapy workshops and patterns get quilters into the habit of cutting down and organizing their scraps into those same "sensible" sizes, which form the basis for her quilt designs.

Similarly, Bonnie Hunter developed the Scrap User's System of predetermined square and strip sizes that are compatible with common block patterns. The ScrapTherapy and Scrap User's System methods share a couple of underlying principles. First, you need to spend time trimming your scraps into useful, same-size pieces and then sort them by color. Then go crazy and sort them even further by value and intensity within the same hue. Box them up for easy retrieval.

Nancy Arseneault uses the Scrap User's System techniques to trim her scraps into consistent sizes.

Photo by Nancy Arseneault

Nancy Arseneault also cuts strips into predetermined lengths to make it easier to use the scraps in later projects.

Photo by Nancy Arseneault

> Cut scraps into useful, same-size pieces and then sort them by color in separate containers.

Collecting scraps is a lot like eating: everything in moderation.

Dumpster Diving, Scrap Bin Style

The thought of precut scraps in neat stacks for easy selection is enough to give any professional organizer goose bumps and the chills. The trade-off is giving up the adrenaline rush that comes with dumpster diving through a plastic bin overflowing with scraps.

Sort by Color in Boxes

If you know now that precutting your scraps just ain't gonna happen, an alternative could be to box up your scraps by color. This makes finding the right color for appliqué and crazy patches easier.

In Shoe Pockets

If your scraps are consistently minimal and you use them often, try stuffing them in color-coordinated bunches into over-the-door shoe pockets or hanging mesh compartments.

Definitely No Scraps!

Not interested in scraps at all? Sell them on eBay or Etsy. Take them along to a guild meeting, or tie them up in a larger piece of fabric and gift them to a new quilter who will just love you for sharing. If worse comes to worst, throw them away and just be done with it.

Store scraps in an over-the-door shoe-pocket organizer.

STRIPS AND STRINGS

Strips and strings are narrow and long pieces. If you don't keep a lot of them, you might be able to get away with draping them over coat hangers hung on over-the-door hanging racks or on a closet clothes rod. There are also cleverly designed trouser hangers that fit in the doorjamb, hiding them behind the door. If you use any kind of trouser hanger with multiple rods, you can sort the strings by color.

If you have floor space to spare, you'll get a pretty fabric display by folding strips and strings over the rungs of a clothes-drying rack, a wood ladder, or a free-standing pant trolley. When the strips overlap each other on the rungs, blocking out the lower layers, it's time to start string piecing or making your next strip quilt.

SELVAGES

Whether or not selvages get your creative pulse racing, you still have to deal with them after you trim your yardage. You can add them as stuffing to an open-ended pet bed pillow, or you can store them until you need them for a totally adorable craft.

A fun way to store them is to roll them into cylinder shapes or into small balls, tie them off or pin them, and toss them into a large pickle jar. Displayed prominently in your quilting studio, the jar will look like a million bucks in between matching barrel jars filled with buttons, embroidery floss, and rolls of bindings.

BINDINGS

As we will discuss in Chapters 5 and 6, it can be very convenient to store all the makings of a quilt top, including cut pieces, finished blocks, and even the pattern and fabric snips, in a plastic satchel like the ones from ArtBin (page 84). If you already have your binding selected or cut, add it to the case to keep all the ingredients together.

For longer-term storage or a more artful display, bindings can be just as striking as selvages when rolled and stored in a barrel jar.

Use a trouser hanger to organize strips.

Display your selvages while you collect them for crafty creations.

LESS THAN SCRAPS

When you emerge from a frenzy of scrap cutting, what do you do with the trimmings? Stuffing! Puppets, pincushions, ragdolls, or whatever else you can dream of stuffing with the snippings and clippings.

Scraps make fun craft projects.

Photo by Diana Taylor

I love the initiative of some quilters who have teamed up with their local animal shelters to sew pet pillows.

Stitch together three and a half sides of a pillow cover and start filling it with the teensiest of trims and threads. Before you know it, you will have a fully stuffed pet bed ready to donate. Give those snips and scraps one last chance at serving a dutiful purpose.

Still, nothing beats using up your scraps in craft projects, scrappy quilts, or even miniature quilts.

BATTING AND BOLTS

I've seen batting stored in vinyl Christmas tree bags, and in the studio of a longarm quilter, I've seen as many as five rolls of batting still in their shipping boxes. To store batting and bolts, you definitely need space. Another great option is to place them in a shiny new galvanized garbage can.

BATTING

Batting can fill an entire corner of a room or the best part of half a closet. Quilters who quilt for other quilters may have the largest area, second only to that of their longarm machine, dedicated to rolls of various types of batting. If you are considering taking up the business of quilting, be sure to account for the storage space you will need for batting.

An ideal storage location for batting is rolled and standing vertically inside a tall cupboard. If your quantities are smaller, folding batting and stacking it horizontally in a cupboard can be very effective. Be sure to raise or lower the cupboard shelves as needed to avoid wasting space in between. Do your best to separate different batting materials into groups.

Save time finding the right size piece of batting. Use a safety pin to attach a label to each piece, stating the dimensions.

Use Up Batting Scraps

You can use up smaller pieces of the same type of batting by butting them up against each other and sewing them together using a zigzag stitch. Have a craft in mind to use up leftover batting pieces, add them to your pet-bed scrap bags, or get rid of them all together.

Even small batting scraps are ideal giveaways for child-care centers and primary schools, which can use them for a multitude of craft projects. Perhaps it would be even more thoughtful to gift the school the batting scraps together with a couple of accompanying craft project ideas.

Bookcases turned on end make ideal storage for bolts.

Fabritopia owner Jona Giammalva bought ready-to-assemble book-cases with adjustable shelving. She has the bookcases in her studio stacked horizontally three high, with the shelves evenly spaced to hold fabric bolts.

BOLTS

The cleverest fabric-bolt storage options are made for retail businesses. We are all familiar with the display shelves and round tables found in fabric stores. Unless you are a heavy user of fabrics by the bolt, you likely don't need a fancy storage solution.

Store Your Bolts Nearby

If you buy only the occasional fabric bolt, I would be wary of storing it far from your regular stash. Out of sight, out of mind. You are likely to forget that you have the bolt the next time you go shopping through your stash. Instead, find a place near your everyday fabrics, and preferably near your cut fabric pieces of the same colorway.

Store Bolts Vertically for Easy Retrieval

Bolts can be stored either vertically or horizontally. I prefer the look and ease of retrieval of vertically standing bolts. Good vertical solutions are usually shelves in closets or in bookcases that can be adjusted to just slightly above the height of the bolt. You may also have to plan to prop them up against a wall, an edge, or another object to keep them upright.

Cut Up Bolt Remainders

If any of your bolts are lingering relics from projects long since completed, cut them up into fat quarters and gift them to your fellow guild members. Or, mix and match coordinating fabric remnants into your own bundled blends and sell them.

thread, notions, tools, and more

Transforming fabric into art might be what transports you to your own happy place, but every quilter has somewhere between a few dozen and a few hundred tools that all promise to (if not all actually deliver on) make quilting more convenient and efficient. And where do all those tools end up? In the *junk drawer*.

TAMING THE JUNK DRAWER

If your quilting junk drawer is anything like the ones I've seen, it's not nearly as organized as your kitchen junk drawer. To begin with, your quilting junk drawer is probably housed within one of those ubiquitous plastic rolling cart units. With drawers so deep, all your terrific, time-saving quilting tools and gadgets get jumbled together into an intimidating heap. The new stuff buries the old stuff. Before long, you forget what's at the bottom. How's a busy girl supposed to think to use her fancy needle-felting kit if she can't see it? So before we explore ideas to better organize your tools and notions, let's dig into your junk drawer and a couple of other notorious hiding spots to rediscover what notions you already own.

As with any organizing project, begin the sorting process by emptying out the area. *Spoiler alert!* (If you want to know where this is going, I'll tell you. You are removing from your junk drawer the tools and notions that you can better organize in another way. Read on through this chapter for all the ideas. Then, the doodads and incidentals that don't fit into some other category can go back into the quilting junk drawer.)

Deep drawers trap items at the bottom where you can't see and forget you have.

LET'S REVIEW: THE SORTING PROCESS

As we tame the junk drawer, let's review the steps in the sorting process from Chapter 1 (pages 19–27).

- Empty out the area.

- Make a keep / not keep decision about everything.

- Group like items.

- Make more keep / not keep decisions once you see everything together.

- Decide the stations where items go.

- Assess the available storage space in the station.

- Find the right container to match both the size of the grouping and the size of the storage space.

- Put the grouping of items away in its new home.

- Maintain the organization.

GATHER UP ALL THE TOOLS AND NOTIONS

Here we go, hunting for tools and notions … in the junk drawer, around your sewing machine, at your cutting table, and in the various on-the-go bags that travel with you to meetings and classes.

There are two reasons we are kicking off organizing tools and notions by first taming the junk drawer. First, you'll need those tools and notions to implement the new organizing ideas in this chapter. Second, what's left behind once you remove the main tools and notions are the leftover odds and ends that go back into the junk drawer. Fitting them back into a newly organized junk drawer teaches you two very important organizing lessons: the concept of *compartmentalization* and the process of keeping *back stock inventory*.

COMPARTMENTALIZATION

Heap control and prevention happens with compartmentalization. I first introduced compartmentalization as part of the sorting process in Chapter 1. The more you can containerize each group of tools and notions in specific categories, the easier it is to see what you have, to remember you have it, and to find it when you need it.

Use small containers to compartmentalize your drawers. Add cut-to-size pieces of rubberized shelf liner to keep the containers and drawer contents from sliding.

Rubberized shelf liner prevents items from shifting around in a drawer.

tip

Drawer Trays

You can compartmentalize by adding drawer trays of various sizes. You'll find them in the kitchen organization section at a discount retailer.

You may also have a drawer deep and wide enough to accommodate a two-tiered drawer organizer tray on which the top tray slides front to back or lifts off to allow you to reach contents below. Or, use lidded or stackable containers that can support a top tier.

Repurposed Containers

Use any repurposed containers, such as empty (and clean) food packaging or GladWare. Try lidded plastic baby-food containers for small items such as thimbles or embellishments. I always recommend transparent containers so that you can easily see into them. But when it comes down to it, the key to using the tools and notions you already own is to compartmentalize your stuff using whatever containers get the job done.

Compartmentalize deep drawers using drawer dividers or stackable food containers.

CREATE A BACK STOCK INVENTORY

Take a look at your junk drawer in your quilting studio. Does your drawer boast two lint rollers and a complete six-pack of roller refills? How about two rolls of bias tape, one opened and the other unopened?

Removing the *back stock*—the items you have bought to replace ones that run out—does wonders for clearing out the junk. Keep just one of everything handy and place the extras in a plastic crate or bin that fits neatly into a nearby cupboard.

When you run out of tape, take the next roll out of the crate of back stock. Take the last tape out of the crate? Put tape on your shopping list. Keep your shopping list current and stick to the list to avoid duplicating purchases and overstocking supplies.

Set up back stock inventory control. Gather up all your duplicates and extra supplies and place them in a plastic crate for easy access. When you run out of a supply, shop your back stock first to use up what you have already bought. Then replenish your back stock when you take the last one of a given item.

THREAD AND BOBBINS

Organizing thread involves four primary considerations:

1. Size of spool or cone
2. Fiber type
3. Use
4. Color

Since spool size can vary greatly from one manufacturer to the next, you need to look for other differentiating criteria to be able to avoid the jumble of a drawer or box full of assorted threads.

KING SPOOLS AND JUMBO CONES

Begin with the size of the spool and matching wound bobbins if you have them. Separate the king spools and the jumbo cones, for example. If they aren't already on thread stands that hold an array of 10 to 20 colors at a time, these cones and king spools can be stored upright in sturdy drawers. Consider inserting a thread tray into the bottom of the drawer to keep the cones in place.

Ready-made thread cases or trays , like this one from ArtBin, hold king spools and cones in place for easy inventory and matching.

To prevent the cones from unraveling, slide the original plastic wrappers back on or use thread nets.

Thread nets keep your jumbo spools from unraveling.

Coats & Clark offers a clever Button Wrap Top, which is a color-coded disc that tops its mini-king cones to denote the fiber type. Eliminate the guesswork and quickly organize your cones by fiber type. You could also compartmentalize your drawer so polyester spools occupy half the drawer while rayon spools occupy the other half.

THREAD SPOOLS

With the cones and king spools separated, divide the remaining thread spools by fiber type: cottons, cotton blends, polyesters, rayons, silks, metallics, and so on. Once you observe your collection by type, it naturally follows that you can look at your threads by use, such as hand quilting, machine quilting, or embellishment. At this point, you can consider racking your spools.

Wall Racks

I love wall racks because they look so fantastic. They're striking and colorful and can possibly provide more visual bang for the buck than other kinds of wall art in your quilting studio. You should mount your thread rack to a wall that doesn't get direct or indirect sunlight and is within easy reach of your machine.

If you have enough empty wall space to have multiple racks, dedicate a section of each rack to spools of a different fiber type. Racks are available in different sizes, so you might have an extra-large rack of cottons but only a mini rack shared by silks, high sheens, and metallics, for example.

Be sure to protect your racks from direct sunlight. tip

Table-stand racks are also available, but I recommend that you diligently keep your table surfaces free from clutter and give yourself more room to work by using wall-mounted racks.

Wall racks serve to organize different thread types while adding a big splash of color to your quilting space.

Storage Boxes

Another storage solution for thread that I have seen work well is to hang Sulky's Slimline Storage Boxes from their handles on pegboard hooks or tuck them onto a shelf under the sewing table. Sulky also offers a Universal Slimline Storage Box that fits spools of varying sizes. Other thread manufacturers such as Coats & Clark sell storage cases, some of which are already kitted with a variety of quality threads—a great idea for beginning quilters.

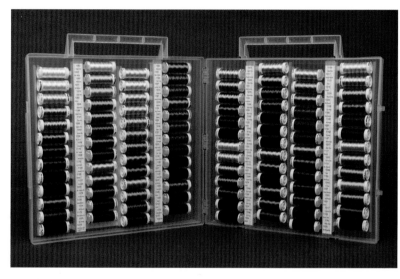

Photo by Andrew Kornylak, courtesy of Sulky

Sulky Slimline Storage Box

Photo by Claudia Lopez, courtesy of Sulky

Arrange by Color

The final opportunity for organizing your threads is sorting by color. Whether you like the ROYGBIV (red, orange, yellow, green, blue, indigo, violet) order of spectral colors or its VIBGYOR inverse, arrange your threads in rows by color.

If you think in terms of a grid pattern and apply the color concepts of hue, value, and intensity, you can create a fancy arrangement by sorting spectral colors horizontally by *value* (lightest to darkest) and vertically by *intensity* (brightest to dullest). Organizing your thread racks can be great hands-on practice toward mastering color matching to inspire eye-popping color combinations.

Arranging your thread by value and intensity helps you create stunning color combinations.

BOBBINS

Bobbins can sometimes be like stepchildren to thread spools; they get a little overlooked at times. I know a lot of you quilt with neutral threads on your bobbins, which means that you probably don't have an abundance of wound bobbins scattered around in your drawers and on your sewing table. For those of you who like color variety and matchy-matchy bobbin threads, you can keep bobbins together with their coordinating thread spools using an organizer made for that purpose or by inserting a golf tee through both holes of the bobbin and then through the top of the thread spool.

ArtBin makes a translucent plastic bobbin box that holds about 30 bobbins. You might also like the BobbinSaver flexible rubber ring from Blue Feather Products as your bobbin storage solution. Store the bobbin box or rubber rings in a shallow drawer or hang the rings from a pegboard hook, being careful to keep all your threads out of direct and indirect sunlight.

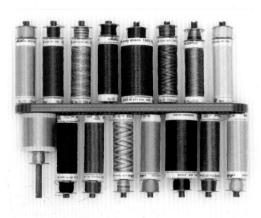

Spooler from Feather King

Photo courtesy of Feather King

A flower pincushion adorns the golf tee that keeps the spool and matching bobbin together.

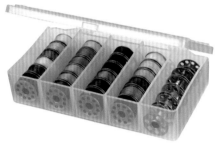

Bobbin box

Photo courtesy of ArtBin

BobbinSaver

Photo courtesy of Feather King

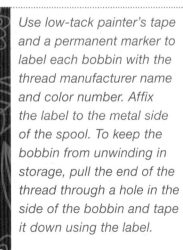

Use low-tack painter's tape and a permanent marker to label each bobbin with the thread manufacturer name and color number. Affix the label to the metal side of the spool. To keep the bobbin from unwinding in storage, pull the end of the thread through a hole in the side of the bobbin and tape it down using the label.

tip

Make labels with the thread manufacturer's name and color number for your matching bobbins.

PINS AND NEEDLES

STRAIGHT PINS

I have seen no better combination for pin storage than the original packaging or a magnetic pincushion. Magnetic pincushions like the Grabbit hold your pins in place without harming any nearby computerized sewing machines or electronics. I can also think of a half-dozen uses around the house for a magnetic pin wand, besides corralling pins that strayed from appliqué or pieced projects. Try the Sweep Magnet from Lehigh Group. Or, equip yourself with both.

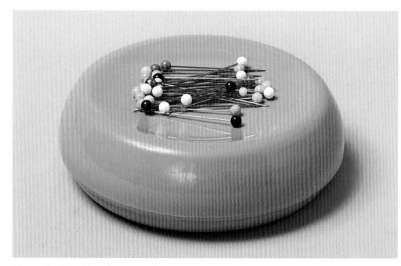

Magnetic pincushions keep pins from escaping.

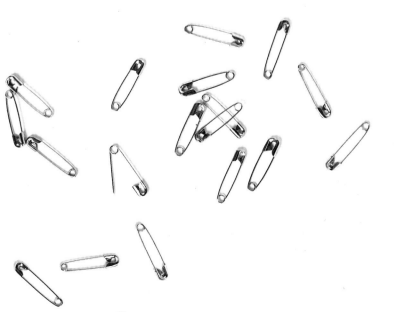

BASTING SAFETY PINS

Whether they use plain old safety pins, curved basting pins, or safety pins paired with Quilters Delight safety-pin grip covers, do quilters ever actually exhaust their supply of basting pins? Because the pins somehow migrate gradually to the same mysterious place as lost socks, you will eventually run out of basting pins. Keep your back stock in tightly lidded, translucent boxes.

Keep your back stock of pins in tightly lidded, translucent boxes.

> *Use translucent boxes whenever possible. You are more likely to remember what and how many you have if you can see them. Matching food containers work well because they nest together when empty and stack easily when full.*
>
> tip

NEEDLES

The trick to keeping your machine needles organized is knowing exactly what size they are. Do your best to keep needles in the manufacturer's original packaging. You can store those packages together in a tightly lidded, translucent box in your back stock crate. Or, you can slip the packages into binder pages made for trading cards or into a compact 4″ × 6″ photo album.

Once you have used a needle, always keep it separate from new needles. Paint the tops of used needles with nail polish to distinguish them from new ones.

You can also keep used but still sharp needles in a pincushion labeled by needle size.

Touch up the tips of hand quilting or machine needles using an emery strawberry. Collect used needles for disposal in a securely lidded pill bottle to avoid injury.

tip

Alex Anderson keeps her used but still sharp needles in this pincushion labeled by size. Reprinted from *Machine Quilting by Alex Anderson.*

If you often quilt on the go, you probably need to keep a small stash of needles in your bag. I have not seen an organizing solution cuter or more useful than handmade needle cases. Look for a needle case project you can make (using up scraps!) and be sure to stitch in numbers for needle sizes.

CUTTING MATS

You may need to bore holes into your cutting mats if you hang them on pegboard. But no holes are required if you clip your oversized cutting mats into trouser hangers and then store the hangers from an over-the-door hook. If the back of the door is too far from where you cut, try hanging the mat from a heavy-duty 3M Command hook beside your cutting table.

Trouser hangers keep oversized cutting mats out of the way behind a door or on a wall.

SMALL TOOLS

There are several must-have tools that you just can't put farther than arm's reach from your machine. These essentials include your shears, thread scissors, seam ripper, tweezers, marking pencils, lint brush, stiletto, and so on. Of course it's convenient for these types of tools to be lying on your sewing table, ready and waiting. But they're bound to get lost under fabric, patterns, blocks, magazines, and today's leftover lunch.

> Take the extra five seconds to put your tools back where they belong instead of allowing them to contribute to the heap. No kidding! Five extra seconds to put something back when you are done can make the difference between tidy and cluttered.

PEGBOARD

If you don't already have pegboard installed on at least one wall of your quilting space, make a call to your favorite handyperson right this very minute. This is a fabulous organizing system that is particularly well suited for your cutting tools, rulers, and mats.

In small rooms, pegboard can take advantage of wall space instead of cluttering up limited tabletop space or drawers. When space is at less of a premium, Some quilters have remarkably large pegboards on their walls that are home to just about every tool, ruler, and cutting mat they own.

Your hardware store will sell a variety of hooks and pegs that will let you hang just about anything from your pegboard. Hanging your tools also prevents the dulling that comes from banging around in a drawer or among smaller tools in a canister.

Pegboard keeps your must-have tools accessible and visible and limits dulling from other forms of storage.

Another hanging option for your metal tools such as shears, stilettos, tweezers, and thread cutters is to store them on a magnetic knife holder mounted to the wall.

A magnetic knife holder mounted to the wall above your cutting table also keeps tools accessible without dulling them.

Photo by Nancy Ansenault

CONTAINERS

For small tools, such as your seam ripper, stiletto, tweezers, mini screwdriver, sewing machine brush, thread clipper, or Kwik Klip safety-pin fastening tool, use a common coffee mug / tea tin approach.

For more pizzazz than a coffee mug, try repurposing a picnic utensil basket or a utensil basket made for a dishwasher.

Tool Caddies

Where your essential tools belong is in the (compartmentalized) drawer of your sewing table or in a tool caddy on your table surface. Tool caddies are very popular with scrapbooking enthusiasts. Look for portable caddies with plenty of pockets and pouches to keep your stuff separated. Not only will your blades and tips stay sharper, but you will also avoid the temptation of dropping small items into the dark abyss of the coffee can that currently stores your shears and pencils.

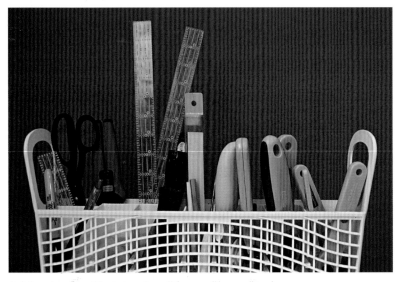

A dishwasher utensil basket works well for corralling small tools.

Tool caddies offer visibility, portability, and compartmentalization.

Table Easels

If you have enough sewing table surface to spare, you might like a table easel, such as the one from ArtBin, that holds tools in rows of elastic loops on both sides of the A-frame stand. Each tool gets its own loop, and all the tools are readily visible. With this easel solution, you'll see at a glance which tools are still missing in action, so you can get them back where they belong.

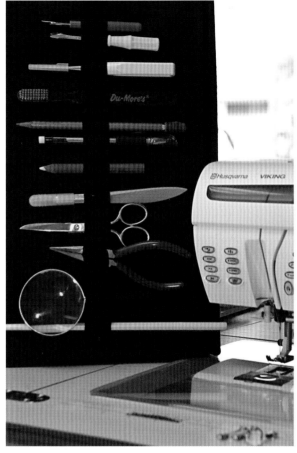

Rows of elastic loops keep your tools within reach at your work surface. The stand is easy to fold and pack, too.

Canvas Totes

I like portable canvas totes. The various pockets make it easy to keep everything within reach, and I can move it anywhere. Just be sure that you keep your basket of small tools *small*. Keep tabletop clutter to a minimum. Remember, you want more room to quilt!

Cropper Hopper Tote-ally Cool! Tool Caddy

Keep tabletop clutter to a minimum. You want more room to quilt!

If you are quilting in a compact space or need a clever hanging solution at a station for just a couple of tools, look to a manufactured set of hooks for cups or keys.

Cup racks and key racks usually offer a series of hooks along a small board that you can mount conveniently at your sewing or ironing station. Try using key hooks or bigger hat racks for storing hoops on an unused bit of wall.

If you need just one hook for a certain spot, I like 3M Command hooks with removable tape.

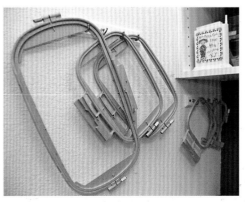

Hooks made for keys, cups, or hats can be a charming solution for storing small groups of tools, hoops, or rulers.

FABRIC PENCILS AND MARKERS

In the pencils and markers category, I wouldn't be at all surprised if you have some purging to do. It takes some trial and error to find a reliable brand of fabric-marking tools that draw easily visible lines, sharpen to a fine point, don't rub off, and wash out as they are supposed to. If you have experimented and have been at all disappointed with the performance of any of your fabric pencils and pens, it's high time to let those go.

QUALITIES OF GOOD FABRIC-MARKING PENS:

- They glide easily.

- They sharpen into a fine point.

- Their marks don't rub off too soon.

- Their marks disappear according to the manufacturer's instructions.

What to use to contain your pencils and markers, you ask? Ye olde tin cup never seems like a bad idea. I still love to use the découpaged tea tin my daughter made in Mrs. Gleason's prekindergarten class. Choose something that you find beautiful or inspiring. Even better, your container for fabric pencils and markers should be transparent, so that you don't forget that you dropped your needle threader or stray buttons into the dark abyss of the container. Or, set a desk organizer tray right into your shallowest sewing table drawer and arrange in it your trusty fabric pens and markers and other must-have notions.

A transparent container prevents other items from being lost and forgotten at the bottom.

RULERS AND TEMPLATES

A new quilt pattern may boast new dimensions and configurations that inspire you. But the new angles might also ignite your maniacal fear of wonky corners and misaligned seams. It's not my place to judge whether every new pattern beckons for a new ruler, but that seems to be the running theme in explaining ruler creep. To keep your rulers at the ready for those most challenging cuts and folds, I must give you the one rule of ruler storage: no stacking them in a drawer!

A drawer stacked full of rulers is just a useless mass of expensive but indiscernible acrylic. If you paid good money for a ruler, at least remember that you already own it. I implore you to store your rulers separately.

RACKS

My favorite storage method for rulers is to place them in the slatted wood racks made specifically for rulers. I recommend mounting them to the wall, so you keep your surface space clear.

Slatted ruler racks keep rulers visible and accessible. This custom rack boasts a compartment behind it to house cutting boards and large rulers.

Photo by Nancy Arseneault

PEGBOARD

Another clever storage solution is to hang rulers from a pegboard wall: one ruler per hook. Pegboard is *so* useful.

VERTICAL DRAWERS

As part of the redesign of her studio, a quilter I know named Gail installed both upper and lower kitchen cabinets along one wall of her room. She specifically added a vertical drawer to her row of lower cabinets. When installed in a kitchen, this same vertical drawer would normally hold cookie sheets, baking trays, and cutting boards upright. She applied this same idea to store her self-healing mats on one side of the pull-out drawer and her rulers on another.

A vertical drawer originally designed for a kitchen is part of the built-in cabinets in this quilting studio.

MACHINE ACCESSORIES

Organizing machine accessories involves telling the truth. As a general rule, accessories for your sewing machine are awkwardly sized, difficult to store, and seldom used.

If you bought your machine because of its fancy array of useful accessories, or if you bought the extras thinking that the devices could take your art to new heights, you need to be realistic about their actual usefulness to you. Intending to use them doesn't mean you necessarily ever will. Keep that in mind as you look at all your machine accessories.

PRESSER FEET

The first place you might look to store your presser feet is within your sewing machine. Some machines are cleverly designed with built-in storage compartments for important (but small) tools such as bobbins and presser feet.

Another storage solution I saw in the classroom at one of my local quilt shops was a divided snap-lid case. I recommend Snapware's layered craft Snap 'N Stack storage containers. To prevent the presser feet from rolling around inside the slick plastic containers, try trimming some rubberized shelf liner to size and laying it on the inside bottom of each container layer.

This stackable container conveniently keeps machine accessories subdivided.

THROAT PLATES

Divided snap-lid cases are also great for throat plates. Again, you might minimize the rattling of your plates in their containers by lining the container bottoms with cut-to-fit pieces of shelf liner.

Another option is to slip each throat plate into a labeled zippered sandwich bag, so you know which plate belongs to which machine. If you ever decide to part with your current machine, you can quickly sort through the labeled throat plate bags and send off the machine to its new owner with all its correct parts.

Label your machine parts with the make and model of the machine.

tip

EXTENSION TABLES

Extension tables might be the most awkward of machine accessories to store. They are bulky and incongruously shaped, making them difficult to store. Always start organizing with your plan in mind, knowing how often you use each item you own and from where it can be conveniently retrieved.

If you don't pack up your machine very often to hit the road and sew, your machine's travel case might be an ideal storage container for the extension tables.

If packing and unpacking the extension tables from your travel case every time you want a change of scenery is too much of a hassle, you might consider finding a clear plastic storage bin that fits one or more of your extension tables. When they are in a bin, you can at least turn those oddly shaped tables into uniformly rectangular shapes that you can label with the make and model of your machine and then stack high on a closet shelf until you next need them.

HOOPS

If you use your hoops often, you need to keep them within easy reach. It's probably no surprise that I am going to suggest hanging your machine or hand embroidery hoops on—you guessed it—a pegboard wall.

If pegboard really isn't your style, try hanging the hoops from decorative wall hooks. You might even have enough depth on the inside of a cupboard door to hang the hoops from removable 3M Command hooks. You can dampen the noise of the hoops clunking against the back of the door by adding felt dots like those made for protecting furniture legs.

If you don't use your hoops often, perhaps you can add your machine hoops to the same container you selected for your extension tables and store them together.

BUTTONS, RIBBONS, AND EMBELLISHMENTS

Second only to your fabric, your embellishments are your prettiest collection. Glass jars filled with assortments of buttons, zippers, embroidery floss, ribbons, sequins, beads, and charms—how charming.

Glass jars turn your embellishments into eye candy.

GLASS JARS

If you have little gems like these, do your best to show them off. Take advantage of their whimsical look and place embellishment-filled jars on wall-mounted floating shelves or on perimeter shelving just below the ceiling.

The drawback of collecting your embellishments and jumbling them all together in jars is exactly that: jumble. If you don't use your stores very often, then putting them into service as eye candy is a good idea. But if you need those buttons or embroidery flosses pronto, you'll have to take the jars down, pour out the contents, and sort out what you need. Be sure to do that on a serving tray or into another tall-sided container to avoid spilling small embellishments all over the place.

PLASTIC ORGANIZER BOXES

There are also many wonderful organizers made specifically for certain embellishments, such as this floss organizer from ArtBin.

Floss organizer

Photo courtesy of ArtBin

FOOD CONTAINERS

Disposable plastic food containers are great for storing groups of items inside drawers and on shelves. Food containers stack nicely, and you can see what is inside reasonably well. For the smallest items, such as pins, thread cutters, thimbles, and sequins, try lidded baby-food containers. After you eat up the ultrapureed fruit or veggies, you can put the small containers to work.

Lidded food containers are great for compartmentalizing groups of little items.

SPICE CONTAINERS

Plastic or glass spice jars can also make an attractive display out of your smallest embellishments and notions. Mount spice racks to your wall or opt for the magnetic spice canisters that hold to magnetic wall strips or to metal surfaces. I like the selection of tin shapes and sizes at CustomMagneticSpiceRacks.com.

Magnetic containers

Use a label maker to print out adhesive labels for your storage containers. The look will be even sharper if you keep all the font sizes the same.

DIVIDED CRAFT BOXES

A similar solution on a larger scale is to look for a divided craft box or a fishing tackle box with divided trays. ArtBin manufactures a very broad range of storage boxes with crafters in mind. Get out your measurements and find a box that exactly fits both your space and your stuff.

Keep in mind that adjustable compartments are good for creating custom sizes, but tiny items such as sequins and seed beads tend to slip underneath the compartment dividers.

PLASTIC ZIP-TOP BAGS

For storage on the smallest scale, try putting items into plastic zip-top bags. These small bags commonly hold one or two extra buttons on new garments. Reuse them for beads and embellishments and then pack several bags together into a lidded baby food container. No more loose embellishments or wayward notions.

Zippered plastic bags keep embellishments contained.

Don't let loose ends of ribbons and tapes get away from you. Tape, clip, or pin the ends.

SCRAPBOOK STORAGE

For even more storage ideas for embellishments, check out the scrapbooking world, which is full of fun and innovative storage solutions. Plus, it's a little thrilling to shop in different aisles. Look for ribbon spool rods, ribbon boxes, envelopes, bags, tins, jars, pails, bottles, and vials in all kinds of materials and sizes. Choose as many transparent containers as you can find, so you always see what is inside.

STABILIZERS AND FUSIBLES

For an ideal storage solution for rolled stabilizers and fusibles, think of your favorite technique for storing wraps and foils in the kitchen. You will probably like a similar solution for your stabilizers and fusibles.

If you have shelf or tabletop surface space, you could look at one of the compact kitchen racks made for stacking several rolls of wraps and foils. Other horizontal storage options for tabletops and shelves could be shoe organizer cubbies or wine racks. For vertical choices, try standing up your rolls in a small wastepaper basket or in a wine tote. Label each cubby or slot to help you quickly locate the right roll and put it back where it belongs.

Clever solutions for maximizing your storage space while keeping your surfaces free of clutter also include kitchen-wrap racks that screw into the backs of cupboard doors. Or, use an under-shelf basket that grips the shelf above to create a narrow hanging basket beneath.

Nancy Arseneault uses a kitchen paper towel holder mounted to the wall and a CD rack on the table to hold her rolls of stabilizers and other wraps.

Photo by Nancy Arseneault

tip

Heat- and wash-away stabilizers tend to stiffen with prolonged exposure to air. Preserve them in sealed storage bags.

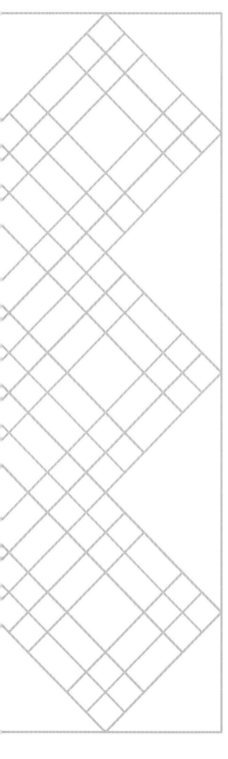

PATTERNS

It's hard to beat the purpose-made pattern boxes made of cardboard. But another option is to divide the drawer of a standard filing cabinet in half. Place two boxes (20″ long × 5½″ wide × 9″ high) side by side in the drawer. This should hold approximately 100 patterns.

However, if you insist on keeping up your terrible habit of saving every free pattern you have ever received from a quilting magazine, you might have a challenge fitting large quantities of oversized paper patterns into organizational systems intended for standard-sized patterns.

Instead, tear out a picture of the finished quilt from the magazine and slip it into a self-closing or top-loading sheet protector. Slip the pattern and any appliqué shapes, instruction pages, and sizing charts behind the picture. Then place the sheet protectors in a three-ring binder.

Tear out magazine ideas and store them in plastic sheet protectors in three-ring binders.

Separate the pattern types with extra-wide divider tabs. Be ultraspecific with your divider tabs so you can quickly find your ideas again. Tab labels can be any mix of quilt types, block types, techniques, project types, gift occasions, fabric types, and so on.

BOOKS, MANUALS, AND MAGAZINES

BOOKS

Quilting and crafting books, by nature, multiply faster than rabbits. One day you buy a new bookcase—and shazam! The next day it's full.

Books are excellent for getting your creative juices flowing. They inspire you and guide you and educate you. But if for any reason a book doesn't do any of those for you, let it go. Sell it to a secondhand bookstore, start a lending library within your guild, or package it up with matching inspirational fabrics you won't ever use and just give them away.

You don't have to organize your quilting books like a library, but some level of order can certainly help. There are two best practices for organizing books. One is to arrange them alphabetically by author. The other is to organize them by theme. Or you can create your own hybrid of themes mixed in together with favorite authors. Whichever you choose, the most important thing is that you enable yourself to use what you have by making sure you can find the right books whenever the creative fire wanes. Browse your favorite books frequently and give up some you don't use to make room for books like this one that you will use often in the years to come.

MANUALS

Magazine holders are also great for keeping all your machine instruction manuals and warranties together or for storing papers, patterns, and idea pages.

For all of you EQ users and longarm quilters, you are likely to have a pile of manuals, CDs, and DVDs that you keep in your quilting studio. Store them in magazine holders and place the magazine holders on a shelf so that their tall spines face outward.

> **tip**
>
> *Face the tall ends of magazine holders outward to give your shelf a cohesive look. Hide the clutter of the magazines, manuals, or papers on the inside.*

MAGAZINES

Books and magazines (in addition to the Internet, quilt shows, and classes) provide trendy insights into the creativity and handiwork of other quilters, fabric artists, and crafters. We love the clever ideas and the fresh fabrics. But show restraint by storing what you truly use.

Rip 'n Read Magazine Pages

If you really do reread magazines cover to cover, then perhaps keep six months of back issues on hand. But if you only read them once, get in the *rip 'n read* habit of tearing inspirational pages from magazines. Rip out the page now and store it in a plastic sheet protector inside a three-ring binder so you can read about the idea again later. Pass on your trimmed-down magazines to quilting friends or recycle them.

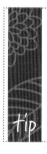

Three-ring binders and sheet protectors are also great for storing appliqué templates or piecing templates.

Refer back to the previous section on patterns to get more ideas on categorizing your ripped pages. Use larger binders for your favorite categories.

File Folders for Magazine Pages

File folders within a filing cabinet can be another effective way to store loose magazine pages. However, it can be a little more difficult to keep the pages together and tidy in a manila file than in a binder (page 77).

Magazine Holders

A favorite storage solution for magazines is upright magazine holders. Magazine holders come in materials ranging from clear acrylic to wood to leather. Lined up in a row, magazine holders make any shelf easier on the eye. They add cohesiveness and a touch of color to your quilting library.

File your magazines by title, by date, or by category. Magazine holders take up more shelf space than the magazines alone, but the upside is being able to pull out just one holder without tipping over the entire stack or having the magazines slip sideways instead of standing up straight.

Magazine holders keep the magazines accessible and attractive.

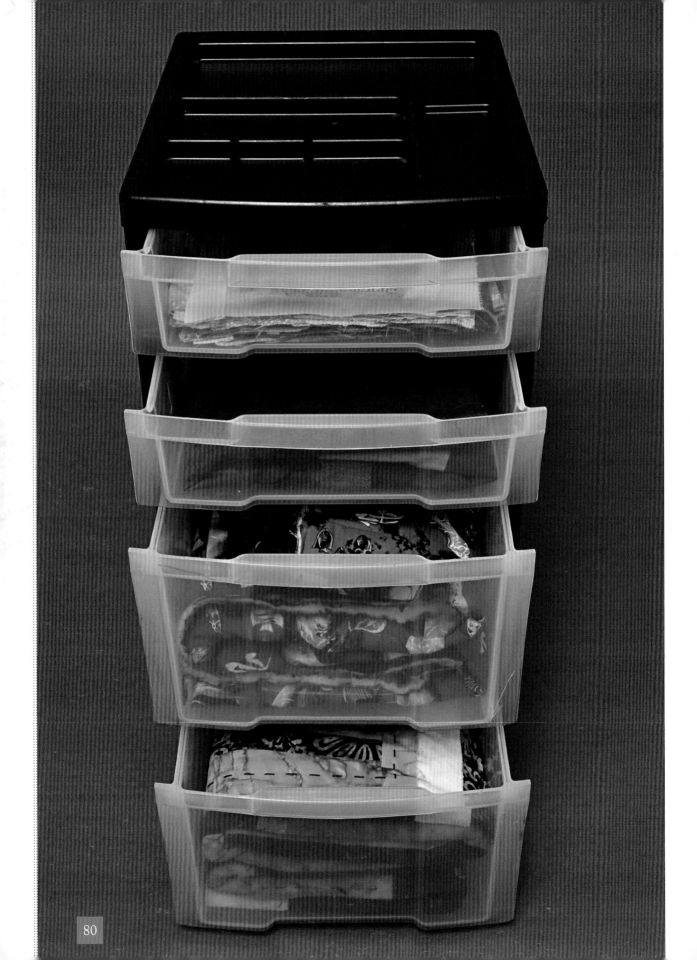

project and ufo storage

Your quilting space is a hub of creativity—a happy place. No wonder it is chock-full of inspiration, with smatterings of class projects, dribs of fabric pairings, drabs of creative stitching, and a healthy dollop of experiments gone wrong. What's a quilter to do?

UFO, WIP, PhD … use whatever acronym you want. They all mean the same thing: unfinished business (hint: UnFinished Object, Work In Progress, Projects half Done). Unfinished business can easily create stress, pressure, guilt, indecision, paralysis, and clutter.

For optimal creativity, let's just be sure that your ideas and projects are not weighing on your conscience and that partially finished projects aren't cluttering up your studio. To deal with these good intentions turned bottlenecks, let's employ the organizing process from Chapter 1.

STEP 1: IDENTIFY THE CAUSES OF YOUR PROJECT PROFUSION

Where do your projects come from? Be true to yourself and truthfully admit what kind of quilter you are. You have to do this in order to create an achievable and maintainable storage system for your quilting projects. Which type are you? Here are a few of the many possibilities. The important thing is to determine why you have so many projects going and try to keep them to a manageable number.

Step 1:
Identify the Causes of Your Project Profusion 81

Step 2:
Set Goals to Deal with the Plethora of Projects 82

Step 3:
Sort Through Your Projects 83

Step 4:
Maintain the Organization 86

Type 1:

You have quilter's ADD and can't stick to a project for more than a day. Embrace it. That's okay. Be at peace with it.

Type 2:

You may need to admit that, like it or not, you are up to your eyebrows in other people's projects, including favors for friends and guild projects galore. Between swaps and circles, you strive to carve out a little time for the other quilts that you dream up for yourself.

Type 3:

You are a true artist. Quilting is one of your many passions. You keep design journals by the dozen, full of swatches, drawings, sketches, words, and general inspiration for past, current, and future art. You study your colors and play with them in a variety of media. You are the quintessential artist in residence, and your studio overfloweth.

Now that you have better insight into how your projects proliferate, you can set goals to help you deal with them. If you are a highly methodical quilter already who doesn't overcommit or underdeliver, you can read ahead to Step 3 (page 83) to get ideas for perfecting your sorting process.

STEP 2: SET GOALS TO DEAL WITH THE PLETHORA OF PROJECTS

Whatever your style, approach Step 2 to determine how best to narrow down your queue of projects based on your real-life quilting habits.

ASSESS YOUR TIME

Begin to set goals for how many projects you can realistically manage by first assessing your time. Be as realistic as possible. How many projects do you typically complete in a month? In a year?

With everything else in your life, do you expect to have more time to quilt? Or less?

What is a good number of projects to have going at once to keep you interested without overwhelming you?

JUST SAY NO

How many quilting projects you have going at once is in large part a result of what you commit to. You might need to say no to new projects. Stop buying magazines for a couple of months. Drive past the quilt shop. Bow out of guild projects for a little while. Politely decline the shop hop. Focus on what you have on your plate already.

ASSESS YOUR INTERESTS

Set additional goals for uncluttering your projects based on how relevant they are to your current quilting style and skills. Do you want to get better at certain skills? Are your ideas becoming more complex or ambitious? Use these thoughts to help you make the tough decisions in Step 3.

OVERCOME WHAT IS STOPPING YOU

If you are stuck on a project that you really do want to finish, identify what the problem is. Is the pattern wrong? Did you make a mistake? Are you encountering a technical difficulty? Do you need to apply a technique you don't know well? Are your original fabric choices wrong?

Once you know the problem, you can set about fixing it. Perhaps ask another quilter for help or take a class to get the skills you need.

Cutting through the clutter and getting your stalled projects moving again improves your organization. Realize that you are freeing up your attitude and your space by tackling a project that had you stumped. One fewer UFO. One more beautiful quilt.

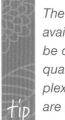

The time you have available to quilt must be consistent with the quantity and complexity of projects you are holding on to.

tip

Overcome what is preventing you from finishing, or let the quilt go.

STEP 3:
SORT THROUGH YOUR PROJECTS

GET IT ALL OUT

Using a folding table or another temporary surface, pull out all your queued projects. Get out a notepad and pen and be ready to make a list.

Look over the assemblage. Now make realistic decisions about what to keep and what to let go. Your backlog of projects, ideas, commitments, and dreams has to match your available time.

What did you find? A half-dozen partial quilt tops? Stacks of mismatched blocks? Takeaways from a bunch of classes? Block swaps you never quilted? Unbound quilts under the guest room bed?

TO KEEP OR NOT TO KEEP?

Weeding out your *I'll-never-do-its* from your *I'll-definitely-do-its* can be heart-wrenching. Saying good-bye to well-intentioned ideas is tough. But there is only one way to get through the projects in your queue. You either have to finish them or get rid of them.

A quilter I respect said that the guilt is in holding on to the UFO, not in letting it go.

Recall Your Original Inspiration

When deciding which quilt projects to keep, remember the ideas that first sparked the projects. Refer back to your design journal notes or remember your thoughts about the patterns, sizes, colors, fabrics, techniques, and time schedules for completion that you had in mind. See if your original plans still excite you.

Give yourself permission to get rid of any experiments or projects that you realistically will never touch again. You learned something from the process of creating them, and they have served their purpose.

If you need even more help in making tough decisions, bribe yourself. Go ahead. Give yourself an incentive to meet your goal: "Today, if I let go of the projects I know I will never finish, I will go get a pedicure." You can even reward yourself along the way for completing projects in your queue. Reward your progress and revel in the feeling of accomplishment while you shed the shame of the *I'll-never-do-its.*

GETTING RID OF THE "NOT TO KEEPS"

Getting back to unfinished business means following your gut. Make decisions based on what you know is right and true. Be ruthless.

I heard a well-respected quilter and teacher say that if you don't like what you have started, you don't have to finish it. So don't.

If the ultimate solution is to let the quilt go, you have a number of options that can help. Take your UFOs to a guild meeting and offer them to the membership, or gift them to a new quilter who wants the practice without the pressure. Know that giving away a UFO not only frees you of a burden, but it also allows someone else to find joy in a project you didn't like.

WHAT TO DO WITH THE "KEEPS"

Collect all the components for each project, such as the picture, pattern, fabrics, embellishments, appliqué pattern pieces, sizing chart, threads, and anything else you need. Once you have them together, keep them together. Project cases keep projects together until you are ready to work on them.

If you aren't going to complete a UFO, pass it along to someone who will. Free up space for something better.

tip

I know quilters who use new pizza boxes to store their quilt projects and to keep them separate. What I don't like about that solution is that you can't *see* what is inside. To jog your memory, label the box well, hang a photo on the front, or tape a fabric swatch to the outside.

Plastic cases with dividers keep projects together.

Pizza boxes are good for storing projects. Label them well so you remember what's inside.

A storage solution I highly recommend is clear flip-top boxes like the 12″ × 12″ double-stack satchels from ArtBin. Use one satchel per project, label it clearly with the project name, and stack it in a visible and highly accessible location. Another similar product is the plastic case offered by the Block Box Company. Seeing what is in your queue can keep you motivated and on track with your project schedule.

Keep your UFOs in transparent containers within plain view of your sewing table. This will help you visually keep tabs on all your great ideas and commitments and prevent you from getting ahead of yourself.

tip

Transparent boxes keep your UFO supplies together and visible so that you don't forget to work on them.

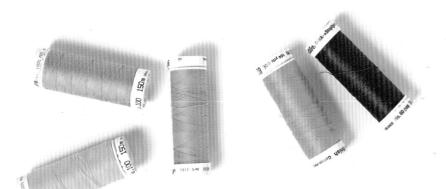

STEP 4: MAINTAIN THE ORGANIZATION

If you just spent a few hours at the cutting table but you aren't going to sew right away, put the cut pieces back in the case or up on the design wall, and then put that case back on the stack. Remember that this is Step 4: Maintain the Organization.

Always be diligent about putting your stuff away when you shift focus to something else. That's the maintenance needed if you want to get and stay organized for good. End the sprawling messes from multiple projects all being out at once.

ArtBin project cases keep projects together until you are ready to work on them. Being able to see all your projects keeps you moving ahead.

Photo by Beth Ferrier

> *Clean up at the completion of every project to make space for the next one. Leftover yardage goes back in the stash. Scraps are saved or tossed. Tools hang on the pegboard. Rulers slide back into the rack.*

tip

HANDLING MULTIPLE PROJECTS AT ONCE

Handling multiple projects at once is very common. Undoubtedly, many of you identified yourselves (page 81) as being "distracted by shiny objects" Type 1 quilters.

You likely wake up in the morning and choose today's project or task based on your mood. You may be in an ironing mood, in a cutting mood, in a holiday fabric mood, or in a scrappy mood. Or, circumstances may change the priority of which project needs attention.

Switching from project to project can certainly keep your creative juices flowing. Just don't forget where you left off on one project when you picked up another. Keep track of your projects and where you are with each one.

Try using a sticky note to write down the stitch count, thread color, and where you left off in case you get interrupted or you put off a project for a while. This can be very useful for hand stitching and embroidery.

> *Time management is about setting manageable goals and realistic timelines.*

USE A PLANNING CALENDAR

Charlene McElroy keeps a fantastic planning calendar that lists, on a grid, all of her dozen or so projects. Projects are listed on the left in rows. Days of the month are listed along the top in columns. Charlene balances her time among multiple projects by marking with an X which days in the month she worked on each one. She uses the calendar to get her blocks of the month done on time and to finish her gifts for each occasion.

If her goal is to complete a project in March, it isn't among the projects on the April calendar. Charlene's system works because she sets *manageable goals* based on the time she has available during the week, and she commits to *realistic timelines* for finishing her quilts. This is a great time management technique you can modify to meet your own style.

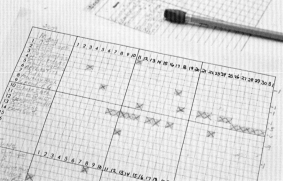

Try using a planning calendar to keep track of your projects and your progress on each.

MAKE NOTES

Quilter and teacher extraordinaire Libby Lehman keeps meticulous track of her projects and to-dos using an arrangement of clipboards hanging on the wall of her studio.

Libby places sticky notes on her various clipboards to track her action items. One clipboard is dedicated to computer work (emails, writing, and website updating). Another tracks the migration of her quilts around the country for various exhibitions and seminars. Yet another lists her personal errands and commitments. Not surprisingly, Libby keeps a clipboard just to keep her on task with her quilting projects.

Libby Lehman keeps herself on task and her projects on schedule by leaving herself notes on the cluster of clipboards hanging in her studio.

Photos by Libby Lehman

IMPROVE YOUR TIME MANAGEMENT SKILLS

Some people are habitually late because they don't actually know how long they need to complete a certain task. To improve your own time management skills in any aspect of your craft-filled life, estimate how long the task will take you. Then start a stopwatch or watch the clock. Write down how long it actually took you compared to how long you estimated.

After a while, you should have a good list of how much time it takes you to iron two yards of fabric, write a blog post, bind a twin-size quilt, call your mother, or hand quilt a table runner. Reference this timing list to help you stay on time and to more realistically set and meet your deadlines.

quilting on the go

Working away from home shouldn't be an exercise in sacrifice and deprivation. But if you are trying to quilt a king-size quilt on an airplane, I'm not sure even a professional organizer can help you. Unless you're seated next to a quilter, I don't expect that either of you will be happy.

We aren't all blessed with oversize quilting studios, either. So we make the best of our limited space and still find sanctuary. This chapter is about quilting with space limitations.

EQUIPMENT FOR WORKING AWAY FROM HOME

Quilters are crafty people. We don't let distance get in the way of quilting. We quilt on the go. So let's pack up and ship out, folks.

The two principles for productively quilting away from home are *compactness* and *portability*. You want your essentials to fit into small spaces (including in the back of your car) and be easy to carry and set up.

ON-THE-GO BAG

By on-the-go bag, I mean whatever catch-all you use to transport your supplies to class or to a friend's house. You probably have more than one favorite bag, depending upon the venue.

Use the bag that best suits your needs, taking into account the time you will spend away from home and the size of the project. But do your best to keep only one set of to-go tools that you take with you, no matter the destination or the bag. We'll talk more about what goes in the bag later.

Keep a list of supplies to replenish. A list can prevent you from overbuying.

tip

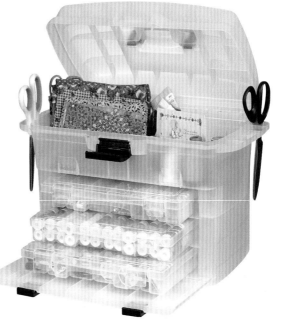

ArtBin Easy View Storage

Photo courtesy of ArtBin

For Schlepping a Lot

If you are still in the market for a durable bag that can accommodate almost any combination of stuff, ArtBin offers a comprehensive line of roller totes and craft bags. Their bags let you pack up tools, fabric, and even your sewing machine all in one. ArtBin's plastic cases also fit neatly into several of their bags, allowing you to pack along your UFOs and other kitted pieces.

Roller tote

Photo courtesy of ArtBin

Sewing machine manufacturers offer a good range of roller bags that can accommodate your machine plus some tools and supplies for quilting on the go.

For Schlepping a Little

Short trips and small projects may only be worthy of a tote bag or a shopping bag.

> *Before you go on vacation, take your machine to be serviced and clear up your work surfaces by putting everything where it belongs. Your room will look so refreshingly uncluttered, and your machine will be ready to go when you get back.*

tip

QUILTING IN THE AIR

Hand quilters and appliquérs have it easy when they are away from home. Throw a small pair of scissors, a few needles, a spool of thread or two, a hoop, and a quilt or fabric pieces into a bag and they're off! Working here, there, and everywhere, you can get a lot of stitching done on the road.

Permissible Tools

If you plan to quilt on an airplane, you should always check the latest information about prohibited items on www.tsa.gov. Scissors with blunt tips or blades shorter than 4" are currently permitted as carry-on items. And so are sewing needles.

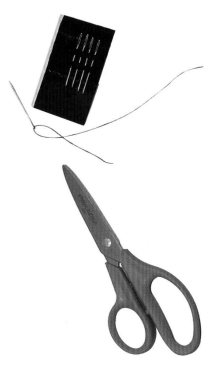

Keep Your Arms In and Stay Seated

Take along a needle case or pincushion to be sure you don't lose pins or needles on the airplane floor. You won't be able to retrieve wayward pins without performing some strenuous physical contortions. And storing your fabric in plastic zip-top bags is never a bad idea for airplane travel, as it can protect from jostling, weather, and spills.

Not that you need to be reminded, but please be a considerate air traveler and always keep your handwork in the bag you place under the seat in front of you. No one wants you opening up the overhead storage bins in flight (ever!) to retrieve your stuff.

Check www.tsa.gov for information about items prohibited in carry-on luggage.

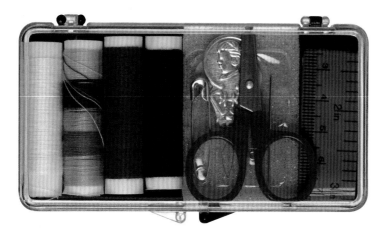

Get into the habit of making a list of supplies you need to replenish, noting whether they are for your on-the-go bag or for home.

TOOLS

When you quilt away from home, should you have one set of tools that stays at home and another set that goes with you? That answer depends primarily on two things. First, will you be more organized if you have a second set of tools always ready? Second, do you have the budget for a duplicate set of tools?

If you opt to have a fully stocked on-the-go bag ready and waiting at all times, buying two sets of tools can be pricey, but I bet there are some duplicate supplies in your back stock (page 60) already. Check before you buy.

tip
Write your name in permanent marker on your tools, so your chances of getting them back at the end of class increase.

Portable Tool Caddy

Since I work a lot outside my home, I compromised by buying all the best tools others had recommended to me, and I keep them stored in a portable tool caddy—at all times. This way, I always have with me what I need, no matter where I am.

A-Frame Stand

The A-frame stand that we talked about in Chapter 4 (page 69) as a tool storage option could also help you stay organized on the go. The elastic loops hold your tools tightly if you want to fold up the stand and take it with you in your tote bag.

Toolbox

The Bob the Builder look might not exactly be your style, but Bob knows a good toolbox when he sees one. Compartmentalized toolboxes do a good job of keeping your quilting tools in order while you travel. I also know quilters who take along fishing tackle boxes for tools and plenty of notions and embellishments.

THE PACKING LIST

To avoid extreme disappointment at finding yourself unprepared, you can create a "packing" list of your favorite tools and supplies, and then refer to that list before you leave to quilt elsewhere.

Suggested Travel Kit Contents

BASIC TOOLS
- Rotary cutter with a new blade
- Rotary ruler
- Rotary mat
- Pencil
- Notepad
- Seam ripper
- Small scissors
- Fabric scissors
- Paper scissors
- Straight pins
- Pincushion or magnetic holder
- Nickel safety pins
- Fabric-marking tool
- Stiletto
- Zippered storage bags

PROJECT
- Instructions
- Fabric
  - Top
  - Borders
  - Backing
  - Batting
  - Binding
- Embellishments
- Specialty rulers
- Specialty tools

MACHINE PIECING OR QUILTING
- Sewing machine
  - Manual
  - Machine tools
  - Bobbins
  - Sewing needles
  - Quilting needles
  - Sewing presser foot
  - Walking foot
  - Free-motion quilting foot
  - Extra bobbins
  - Spare machine bulb
  - Clip-on light
  - Power strip
  - Extension cord
- Thread
  - Piecing thread
  - Quilting thread

HAND PIECING OR QUILTING
- Hoop
- Hand quilting thread
- Thimble
- Needles

IRONING SUPPLIES
- Mini Iron
- Heat-resistant pad or portable ironing board
- Pressing sheet
- Spray starch

Create a "packing" list of your favorite tools and supplies.

CLEVER IDEAS FOR QUILTING IN SMALL SPACES OR ON THE GO

From among all the ingenious ideas quilters have shared for quilting in small spaces, there are a few that stand out for optimizing your comfort. Let's get you set up right—anytime, anywhere.

Look for a 25-foot reeled extension cord with multiple, grounded outlets. Plugging in from a distance and sharing the juice with your neighbor is virtually guaranteed to win you some friends.

A compact iron is perfect for a small space.

If you get stuck on an unforgiving folding metal chair for any length of time, your tush is going to thank you for bringing along a chair cushion or stadium seat cushion. Chair cushions can also help boost you up if the chair seats you too low from the table.

You will inevitably miss the heft of your regular iron when you iron away from home, but you surely won't miss that bulk when you are lifting your stuff in and out of your car. A compact iron can do little jobs in not a lot of space.

A wooden TV tray covered with a cut-to-fit ironing board cover can be a useful stand-in as a pressing surface. Or look for a portable ironing surface that you can use on any tabletop, like the one in the Quilter's Tote from www.junetailor.com.

Another handy alternative could be the Touch Up Topper dryer-top ironing pad that lies out on any tabletop surface, folds up for storage, and uses magnets to adhere to the top of your washer or dryer for a quick press almost anywhere.

A couple of foldable self-healing cutting mats are also on the market. Find one that folds into a size that fits into your on-the-go bag or under the lid of your sewing machine's roller bag. Some ready-made quilt bags, such as the Omnigrid FoldAway totes, include integrated mats.

Make your design wall more portable by keeping a flannel-backed plastic tablecloth in your tote. Quilting teacher Nancy Busby lined the inside of a pizza box to serve as her portable design wall.

Line the inside of a pizza box with batting for a convenient mini design wall.

A small OttLite lamp, a clip-on snake light, or a good book light can transform any dark corner into a productive quilting space. Shop for the highest number of lumens for the smallest size; the higher the lumens, the more powerful the light.

A clip-on book light can add flexible focus in dark places.

PORTABLE STORAGE

Store your project supplies (fabric, thread, patterns, and more) all together for both compactness and portability. ArtBin 12″ × 12″ satchels with divider inserts can be particularly useful for storing blocks in various stages of assembly.

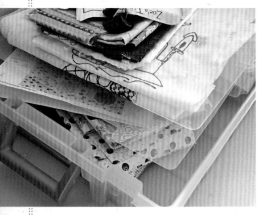

Use a project case to keep cut pieces, finished blocks, pattern, and binding together.

APPLIQUÉ PIECES

I love the idea of pinning appliqué pieces and threaded needles to a piece of batting placed inside a CD jewel case. Slip the jewel case inside the 12″ × 12″ case for the whole project.

A CD jewel case lined with batting can keep appliqué pieces from getting lost.

BLOCKS

Separate cut pieces for each block by placing them in separate plastic zip-top bags labeled with the block numbers. Or, lay pieces for each block between pages of a heavy-weight drawing pad or notebook.

EMBELLISHMENTS

Keep embellishments such as beads, sequins, and charms in tiny plastic zipper bags made for jewelry or in plastic vials.

Plastic zipper bags keep different block types separated when you don't have a big design wall handy.

Zip-top plastic bags keep the tiniest embellishments from getting lost.

Plastic containers separate different types of embellishments.

"WHERE I LEFT OFF … " NOTES

Travel with a pen and a pad of sticky notes to jot down where you left off on your project. This can help you quickly get back to work when you next pick it up.

The more prepared you are for quilting on the go or in small spaces, the more productive you can be. Step back and look objectively at your habits and preferences, and then find organizing solutions that complement your habits. You will get more accomplished in more places.

long-term storage and display

A finished quilt is the culmination of vision, skill, style, time, and love. Whether you own quilts you've made, quilts that others have made for you, quilts you've collected, or heirloom quilts you've inherited, you will want to care for them properly and even take them out from time to time to admire or show them off. Quilts are meant to be used and enjoyed.

Show them the love and attention the quilter originally intended. Put them on your bed, couch, table, wall, or wherever they look most beautiful. Use them. But be sure you understand how best to take care of them.

KNOW YOUR ENEMIES

When you know your enemies, you can be on guard to protect your quilts from harm. The most notorious quilt killers are dirt, pests, temperature, and sunlight. Other harmful agents include common ingredients in household products and cleaners such as alcohol (in hair spray and perfume), oxidizers (in toothpaste and laundry detergents), alkalis (in shampoos and soaps), and acids (in deodorants and hair care products).

To properly store a quilt, your foremost concern is to find a location that minimizes the quilt's exposure to sunlight, pests, dirt, and extreme temperatures. Garages and attics are poor choices. Dark closets and drawers are excellent choices.

If you need to protect your quilts from pests and dirt, use plastic zip-top bags. Archival paper boxes are an even better choice.

*Renowned quilter Diana McClun considers every single exposure of a quilt to sunlight to be **cumulative** damage that can't be undone.*

tip

Even though time is another enemy of quilts, it's just so difficult to stop it. But do your best to eliminate each of these threats in order to preserve your quilts for generations to come.

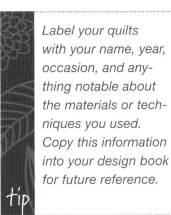

Label your quilts with your name, year, occasion, and anything notable about the materials or techniques you used. Copy this information into your design book for future reference.

tip

STORING QUILTS

Quilts you use regularly as bedding may not require any complicated storage measures. Love them by using them. Quilts you plan to keep forever and ever will require some more careful treatment. Know these rules of thumb to keep them all looking beautiful longer.

REFOLD A STORED QUILT

Quilts are susceptible to permanent creases from folding. Take every opportunity to refold a quilt in a new direction.

In her decades of experience, Diana McClun, co-author of *Quilts, Quilts, and More Quilts!*, has observed that hand-quilted quilts are less stiff and are therefore less prone to permanent fold marks than are machine-quilted quilts. Diana and her business partner, Laura Nownes, are careful to fold their quilts differently every time they pack them.

tip *Refold a quilt in a different direction every time you pack it away. This can prevent the fabric from stretching and weakening along permanent fold lines.*

AVOID STACKING STORED QUILTS

Avoid placing other heavy bedding on top of a quilt when you store it. The other bedding can weigh down the quilt and stress the stitches and seams or create permanent creases.

Use shelf extenders to avoid stacking quilts. Sold in the kitchen and closet storage sections of major retail stores, shelf extenders are like portable shelves that add another surface in between existing shelves. Line the shelf extender with heavy-duty shelf liner or cardboard to prevent grid lines on the shelf extender from imprinting on your quilt.

PROTECT FROM DIRT

If your linen storage closet is in a high-traffic area that could expose the stored quilt in between uses to high amounts of dust, pet hair, or other wear and tear, store it in an unsealed plastic bag. Ziploc's Big Bag product line offers oversized zipper bags that measure up to 24" × 22½". Or, reuse the original zippered plastic bag from a comforter or bedspread.

However, it is important that you don't store quilts in plastic if you don't have to. Fumes, humidity, and mildew can build up quickly in plastic.

Oversize plastic bags can minimize the exposure of everyday quilts to dirt and friction.

Don't store quilts in plastic if you don't have to. Fumes, humidity, and mildew can build up quickly in plastic.

Diana McClun explains her method of storing quilts:

Quilting is my passion as well as my profession. I used to be on the road as often as I was in my Northern California studio, so out of necessity I had to develop organizational storage methods that keep me organized without taking lots of preparation time.

I have four main categories of quilts, and I have a different method for storing each of them because I use the quilts in different ways.

My quilts in progress are my first group. When they aren't out on my sewing table, my current projects are in canvas tote boxes at the bottom of my storage room, where I keep my fabric stash.

Tubular hangers make it easy for Diana and Laura to see and retrieve quilts based on their current patterns.

My partner, Laura Nownes, and I make mostly sample quilts for our pattern line, which are the second category. Because they travel with us a lot for lectures and workshops, we keep sample quilts for our current patterns very handy by hanging them on plastic tubular hangers along the back wall of my studio's storage room. These hangers are thick enough that they don't make permanent creases in the fabric and are convenient for getting the quilts quickly off and on.

In the third category are the quilts that Laura and I have made that are in circulation for trunk shows and exhibitions at guilds and store promotions. They are mostly quilts based on our retired patterns. I store each quilt ready-packed in its own wheeled suitcase. They all live in the climate-controlled loft above my studio.

Every time we get a quilt back from a show, we inspect it, refold it in a different way to avoid permanent creases, and repack it into the suitcase.

Diana and Laura have their trunk-show quilts ready-packed in individual suitcases.

We ship trunk-show quilts in boxes. We lay a sheet of paper on top that describes the care and handling procedures for our quilts. We put these instructions inside for two reasons. First, we want to educate those who borrow our quilts on proper care, such as keeping quilts away from sunlight. Second, we want to make sure that our quilts last a very long time. I believe that all exposure is cumulative. And if I can't reverse damage, I need to try to prevent it.

The last category of quilts I store is my collection of antique quilts. They don't leave my home, so I keep them in a large cedar chest in my living room. I place archival tissue paper between the quilts to prevent any bleeding or leaching from one quilt to another. Although they rarely get brought out or handled these days, I make sure to refold them every time I go into the chest. I ought to admire them more often than I do, so that the love and artistry in these beautiful quilts of yesterday can energize me for the projects I am creating today.

Diana carefully stores her antique quilts in a custom-made cedar chest with built-in shelves to keep the quilts separate.

PROTECTING HEIRLOOM QUILTS

Whether you have inherited an heirloom quilt or made a quilt and intend for it to become an heirloom, you should protect it the best you can.

KNOW YOUR TEXTILES

Know the fiber content of your quilts—top, batting, and backing—so that you can be informed about how best to care for them. If you didn't make the quilt yourself, or if you don't know much about quilts, you should consider paying for a formal quilt appraisal, so you can understand how to care for the materials that make up the quilt. You might be surprised to learn what is between the layers.

Fragile Textiles

Antique silks, hand-dyed fabrics, and quilts with lots of embellishments require special care. Most of these quilts, especially if they are old, should be stored either flat or rolled. Do not stack fragile textiles.

For either method, place the quilt between two pieces of washed muslin. Then, roll the quilt around an archival-quality paper tube. Plan extra storage space for these long rolls.

> "The passion you have for textiles is equal to the care you give them."
>
> — Diana McClun

Quilts with Embellishments

You may also choose to remove any metal pieces or other reactive embellishments from the quilt, but consider including instructions in the storage box for how and where to reattach them. Also be sure to remove all tape and adhesives from stored quilts.

ARCHIVAL STORAGE SUPPLIES

There are a handful of companies that sell *museum-quality archival storage* supplies via the Web and catalogs. Look for *acid-free* archival storage boxes and acid-free tissue.

Archival storage boxes are made of paper to allow items to "breathe" and to prevent damage from contaminants such as acids or plasticizers (PVCs).

Never use plastic bags, boxes, or containers to store your quilts and fabrics for long periods of time. Plastics also degrade over time, becoming more brittle and unstable.

Archival boxes and tissue make an ideal long-term storage solution for heirloom quilts.

Wear cotton gloves to avoid transferring oil and dirt from your hands onto your heirloom quilts.

DIGITAL STORAGE

If you gift your quilts to loved ones or store them away carefully in archival boxes, you can remember what you made and admire what you have packed away in storage through digital images.

Digital images can be simple snapshots you take of the entire quilt top, close-up pictures you take of a block or special design element, or even professionally staged and photographed pictures of your quilts in a special setting, such as in the garden or in the living room.

Think of all the wonderful ways you can preserve your quilts digitally. Anything you can do with a digital photograph you can do with a digital photograph of your quilts.

DISPLAYING QUILTS

For all the time, effort, and thoughtfulness you put into your quilts, give them the public display they deserve. Let your family and friends admire your newest creations as they ooh and aah.

Just know that those to whom you gift your quilts may not feel as free to put the quilts into everyday circulation, preferring to treat them as heirlooms and store them behind closed doors instead. Give your recipients more options for using, displaying, or storing their treasures by advising them on washing instructions, dusting advice, or long-term storage techniques.

AT HOME

On Furniture

A quilt spread lovingly across a bed is a quilt on display just as much as placemats, table runners, and blankets set atop your furniture.

On a Rack

Another traditional display method is the quilt wall rack or floor stand, either of which may accommodate several quilts. Remember to gently dust the quilts often and to refold them each time you lay them back over the rack. Rotate your display based on the season or just to make you smile.

A quilt rack puts your recent creations out for all to see.

On Walls

If the quilts aren't spread across the back of the couch or on the bed in the master suite, they might be adorning the walls. I have seen quilts hanging from binder clips hung from pushpins. Others hang from wall-mounted systems designed especially for quilts.

These wood hangers tightly pinch the quilt into place without damaging the quilt.

Sew a muslin or fabric mounting sleeve onto the back of your quilt just below the binding edge and then hang the quilt from a closet pole, dowel, or decorative curtain rod. Ready-made sleeves are available at www.quilters-hangup.com. Upgrading from binder clips, you might also find clip rings designed to clip up curtains onto curtain rods. Just be careful, because some of them can rust, especially in high-humidity areas.

FOR EXHIBITION

Preparing quilts for competition, professional display, or exhibition can involve a little advance planning. Be honored to be able to share your art with other quilters or the general public.

For more permanent displays, I recommend consulting an archivist with experience in displaying quilts. An archivist or textiles expert can assess the integrity of the quilt and recommend the best method of display given the venue and length of time the quilt is to be shown.

Packing and Shipping

Diana McClun and Laura Nownes keep every one of their trunk-show quilts ready to go in its own rolling suitcase. Give them ten minutes and they can be out the door—impressive.

Care Instructions for Curators

When Diana McClun and Laura Nownes send a quilt for exhibition, they include a written agreement inside the quilt's suitcase, advising the exhibitor of the proper care for the quilt (prohibiting exposure to sunlight, for example) and requiring the curator's signature of compliance.

The pair hopes that this extra step will help preserve their quilts in the long run, which should allow the public to enjoy their art well into the future.

Framing

To exhibit smaller quilts or quilt blocks, consider matting and framing them with archival, acid-free materials. You can choose whether to frame them behind glass or leave the fabrics exposed for frequent admiration and occasional touching. Alternatively, mount smaller quilts onto framed artist canvases. The canvas makes for easy hanging and a professional look.

Pipe and Drape Display

To exhibit large quilts or fabric art pieces, www.hangupscompany.com makes a hook-and-bracket system designed for display at trade shows on pipe and drape systems.

These funky clips hold up quilts in a trade show booth.

Mounting Sleeves

Sewing a mounting sleeve to the back of the quilt can also be effective for hanging large quilts. Or, you could sew the loop side of hook-and-loop tape along the top of a quilt and then mount it to a length of wood with the hook side of the tape attached. The wood can be mounted to a wall with eye hooks.

However you choose to display your quilts, at home or in public, the ultimate goal is to enjoy them. Appreciate the time and love that went into each one. Admire the talent of the artist. Remember the life events that inspired the piece. Share the craft.

Stored safely in a custom-made cedar chest, quilting icon Diana McClun plans to pass on her collection of antique quilts for the next generation to admire. Each layer of quilts is separated by built-in shelves to minimize stress on the old fabrics.

resources

AUTHOR FAVORITES

NOT KEEPING

www.freecycle.org

www.craigslist.org

www.etsy.com

www.ebay.com

FURNITURE

sewing tables

www.hornofamerica.com

www.kangarookabinets.com

www.regalcabinets.com

adjustable chair

www.ergonomicadvantage.com

LIGHTING

www.decoration.com/accessories/interior-lighting

www.ott-lite.com

FABRIC STORAGE

wire mesh baskets

www.closetmaid.com

www.ikea.com

shelf dividers

www.organize.com

www.lillianvernon.com

lidded plastic bins

www.artbin.com

www.sterilite.com

www.rubbermaid.com

www.hpii.com

hanging clothes stacker

www.containerstore.com

bookcases

www.ikea.com

www.sauder.com

www.hermanmiller.com

shoe pockets

www.containerstore.com

www.ikea.com

pant racks, clothes drying racks, or pant trolleys

www.organize.com

www.stacksandstacks.com

barrel jars

Anchor Hocking at retail stores

Libbey at retail stores

THREAD AND BOBBINS

king spools and jumbo cone thread nets
www.threadelight.com

www.abc-machine-embroidery-designs.com

wall racks
www.junetailor.com

www.robison-anton.com

Marie Osmond Elite Essentials

storage boxes
www.artbin.com

www.sulky.com

bobbin storage
www.artbin.com

www.blue-feather.com

PINS AND NEEDLES

Grabbit
www.blue-feather.com

sweep magnet
www.lehighgroup.com

CUTTING TOOL AND MAT STORAGE

pegboard
www.diynetwork.com

magnetic knife holder
www.ikea.com

www.target.com

folding cutting mats
www.dritz.com

wall hooks
3M Command hooks at retail stores

TOOL STORAGE

tool caddy
www.artbin.com

Mackinac Moon at retail stores

Marie Osmond Elite Essentials

table easel
www.artbin.com

canvas tote bag
www.cropperhopper.com

A-frame stand
www.artbin.com

toolbox
www.planomolding.com

RULER AND TEMPLATE STORAGE

slatted rack
www.romwoodworking.com

vertical kitchen drawer
www.closetmaid.com

BUTTONS, RIBBONS, AND EMBELLISHMENTS

glass jars

www.crateandbarrel.com

www.freundcontainer.com

magnetic spice jars

www.custommagneticspicerack.com

label maker

www.brother-usa.com

divided craft boxes

www.artbin.com

zippered plastic bags

www.mileskimball.com

PATTERN STORAGE

filing cabinet organizer

www.birchstreetclothing.com

sheet protectors

Avery at retail stores

MAGAZINES AND MANUALS STORAGE

magazine holders

www.staples.com

PROJECT STORAGE

project satchels

www.artbin.com

CLEVER IDEAS FOR SMALL SPACES

ironing table

www.junetailor.com

www.goldmine.en.alibaba.com

lighting

www.ottlite.com

PORTABLE STORAGE

project satchels

www.artbin.com

plastic zipper bags

Ziploc at retail stores

www.mileskimball.com

canvas tote bags

www.artbin.com

Mackinac Moon at retail stores

Marie Osmond Elite Essentials

toolbox

www.planomolding.com

DISPLAYING QUILTS

on walls

www.quiltershangup.com

www.vjscreativedesigns.com

www.hangupscompany.com

for exhibition

www.hangupscompany.com

QUILT STORAGE

archival storage supplies

www.lightimpressionsdirect.com

www.archivalmethods.com

DIGITAL STORAGE

www.shutterfly.com

www.snapfish.com

www.lulu.com

OTHER STORAGE (FOR ANYWHERE IN YOUR HOME, TOO)

under-shelf storage baskets

www.closetmaid.com

www.containerstore.com

lazy Susan turntables

www.rubbermaid.com

www.oxo.com

plastic containers

www.snapware.com

www.mileskimball.com

www.artbin.com

Glad at retail stores

Gerber 1st Foods at retail stores

Ziploc at retail stores

drawer trays

DV International at www.amazon.com

Rubbermaid at retail stores

rubberized shelf liner

www.duckbrand.com

www.griptex.com

wall hooks

3M Command at retail stores

label makers

www.brother-usa.com

REFERENCE

SEWING HEIGHT AND CUTTING HEIGHT

www.ergonomicadvantage.com

www.osha.gov/SLTC/etools/sewing/ sewingstationdesign.html

ODE TO A STASH, BY BILL MCDONALD

www.blockpartystudios.com

FOLDING FABRIC

thehappyzombie.com/blog/?p=124

Marilyn Bohn, CreativeOrganizer, at www.youtube.com/watch?v=rkTlaMqRlwo

DESIGN BOOKS

www.dickblick.com

www.colormastery.com

SCRAP CUTTING SYSTEMS

www.scrap-therapy.com

www.quiltville.com

PROHIBITED ITEMS FOR AIR TRAVEL

www.tsa.gov

about the author

Carolyn Woods is a professional organizer and a member of the National Association of Professional Organizers (NAPO). She owns Totally Tidy Household Organizing, LLC. She is a frequent speaker on organizing topics at public events and private workshops.

Her humble beginnings as an organizer can be traced back to when, at age ten, she organized office files for her mother's friend in exchange for a homemade lemon meringue pie. In high school, she offered closet organizing services as a summer job. Many years later, when organizing programs premiered on television, Carolyn recognized the market for her natural organizational talents. She established her residential organizing business in 2004.

With two preschoolers at home, Carolyn began her organizing business by focusing on families with children. Most of her organizing work involves helping clients get their bedrooms, kitchens, home offices, and garages under control. She works evenings and weekends with her organizing clients throughout the Phoenix metropolitan area, as she also has a full-time job in marketing communications.

Carolyn has a bachelor's degree in political economy from the University of California at Berkeley and a master's in business administration from Santa Clara University.

A native of California, she now lives in Gilbert, Arizona, with her husband and two children. Her other passions include travel, cooking, reading, scrapbooking, gardening, and hiking with her family.

Great Titles *from* C&T PUBLISHING

Available at your local retailer or **www.ctpub.com** *or* **800-284-1114**